### Ghosts Along the Silk Road...and Beyond

Have you ever wondered if ghosts were all alike, no matter where you are in the world?

### Ghosts Here and There

Mind you, ghosts in the West and ghosts in the East don't seem to be alike at all at first glance, but...

### Ghosts Everywhere

You'll find that some ghosts far away from you have a strange similarity to those close to you. Why is that?

**Take a journey
around the world with us and explore ghosts
wherever you go**

**Workshops by Eilis Flynn and Jacquie Rogers**

*The Silk Road Myths and Legends Workshop Series*
Angels
Demons
Dragons
Faeries
Ghosts
Vampires
Water Beasties
Werewolves and Other Shapeshifters
Bigfeet

The Five Stages of Editing Grief
Geeks and Gamers' Guide to Worldbuilding


**Books by Eilis Flynn and Jacquie Rogers**

Ghosts Along the Silk Road and Beyond

# GHOSTS ALONG THE SILK ROAD AND BEYOND

*Based on the series of workshops presented by*
*Eilis Flynn and Jacquie Rogers*

**Ghosts Along the Silk Road and Beyond**
Copyright ©2018 Eilis Flynn & Jacquie Rogers
Published by Flynn Books Words & Ideas



Original cover design by Jacquie Rogers


ISBN-13: 978-1987710151

ISBN-10: 1987710150




*For Mike and Mark.*
*Thank you.*

# Chapters


*Introduction* • 3

*1* • So Many Things that Go Bump in the Night • 7

*2* • Hooray for Ghostly Hollywood • 11

*3* • Ghosts in the Americas • 25

*4* • Ghosts Across Northern Europe
and the British Isles • 37

*5* • Blurring Lines in Slavic Land • 51

*6* • Greek and Roman Ghosts • 55

*7* • Ghosts in Darkest Africa • 61

*8* • Through the Middle and Near East,
We See Ghosts • 67

*9* • In India and the Subcontinent of Ghosts • 73

*10* • The East Asian Triangle: The Ghosts of China,
Korea, and Japan • 77

*11* • Ghosts, in the Deepest Jungles of
the Pacific Rim • 89

*Summary*
Where Ghosts Are Here and There • 94

*Bibliography and Illustrations* • 96

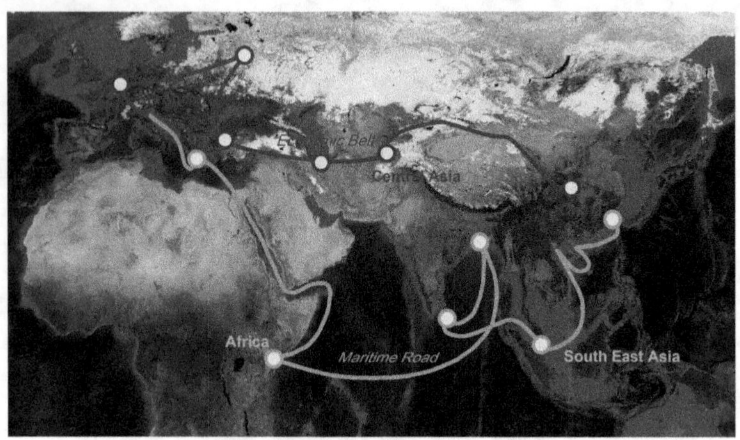


A map for the Silk Road journey.

# Introduction

No matter where you go in the world, take a look at the folktales and the myths in the culture you're in, and more likely than not you'll find a mention of a creature that sounds a lot like one you've heard about all your life. That could be a faery, a dragon, an angel, a demon, or even vampires or werewolves or ghosts. It could even be a story about a sea-based creature that somehow seems unbelievable, yet—not. They can't possibly be true. Right?

Funny thing is, those stories can sound mighty similar to each other, even though they may originate in cultures and places thousands of miles apart. For example, there are stories about dragons in Western Europe, in Asia, and even in Native American culture. They're all different, but judging by the descriptions, they're all clearly dragons. You may dismiss the coincidence, since dragons aren't real (as far as we know), but here's the thing: There are stories and descriptions of such mythological creatures of all stripes and colors all around the world.

This is something that any anthropology major takes for granted, of course. But it's not necessarily something that anybody really thinks about. But that's only because nobody's pointed it out. That's why we're here!

This book was born from a series of workshops when Jacquie Rogers and Eilis Flynn realized there were variations of the same myths all around the world. Eilis was an anthropology major, so she was familiar with the concept that cultures in the same region or came from the same roots would usually have similar legends and myths, and she'd already spent some time studying them, noting how they changed as the cultures did. She was also familiar with Japanese culture, having spent her childhood there. Jacquie had done research on European mythologies for her series of fantasy romances. When we realized that the people around us were always talking about it, we decided to combine all that "book learnin'," as Jacquie would say, and look at the myths along the Silk Road and beyond.

And before we get started, let us tell you about the Silk Road. Traditionally, the Silk Road was a series of important trading routes going over land and sea that existed long before the Christian era began. A *lot* of trade occurred along those routes, bringing silks and spices and more from the East to the West, and vice versa.

The Silk Road connected a region of China with Asia Minor and the Mediterranean, a route that was more than 5,000 miles long—a fair distance these days, but unimaginable back then, fraught with danger and a journey that took a very, very long time for a round trip. The Silk Road had northern routes and southern routes, and the goods were transported from places as far away as the Philippines and Thailand and Brunei, all the way to Italy and Portugal and even Scandinavia.

Not only were silks and spices moved along these routes, so was culture, language, and even technology, and that meant Asian concepts and items were introduced to

Europe, and vice versa. We'll see how those ideas began and changed as we travel from region to region, changing bit by bit until those concepts end up drastically different when compared side by side.

And all that also goes for ghosts.

Ghosts are everywhere, in more ways than you can imagine! Well, maybe you *can* imagine it. We examined quite a few forms of mythological creatures in our journeys along the Silk Road, and it wasn't that surprising that sometimes we wouldn't be able to find a true example. We found that native stories about vampires are scarce in China (the hopping vampire myth was the best of it), while werewolves couldn't be found in native form a lot outside of Europe, faeries by that name were thin on the ground also outside of Europe (but then there were plenty under other names), and there were dragons in many variations, but ghosts … ghost stories can be found anywhere and everywhere. Where there is death, there is a ghost myth. There are feetless ghosts in Japan and hungry ghosts in China and the Americas (complete with festivals to go along with it), a friendly ghost named Casper in American kiddie entertainment, and séances in every culture that has a ghost legend for the living to speak with the dead.

Intrigued? Let us take you on a walk around the world to examine those myths, and see how they shift, change, and evolve as we travel.

Eilis Flynn
Jacquie Rogers

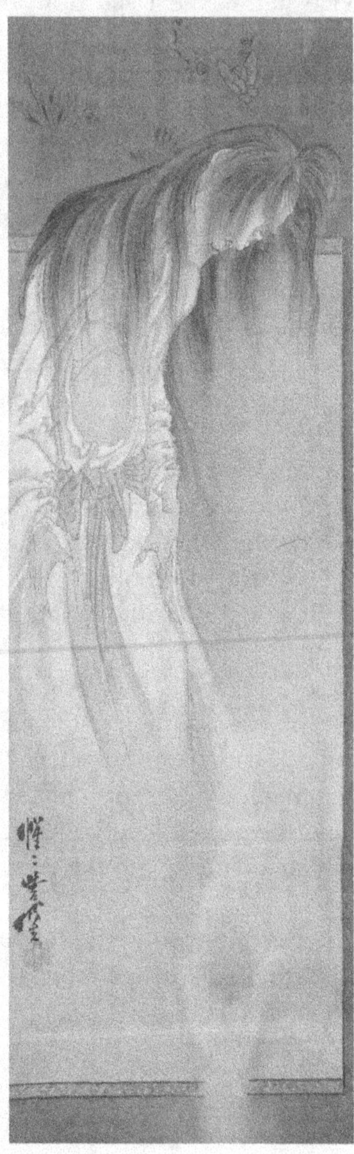

An image of a ghost from a Japanese
woodblock print.

# Chapter 1
*So Many Things that Go Bump in the Night*

Before there were myths and legends about dragons or faeries or werewolves or vampires, there were stories about ghosts. As we mentioned before, ghosts—or more precisely, stories about and the presence of deceased ancestors or others no longer on this mortal plane of existence—have been around since humankind itself has been around. As long as there have been people, people who have witnessed death of some kind, there have been ghost stories.

It's not difficult to say why ghost stories have been around for so long. Death and speculation about what lies beyond life have been the source of fascination for humans from the time that humans started to develop culture. Was it that odd feeling of being watched when there was no one else around, or some sign that a recently deceased relative was somehow, inconceivably, sending a message? While there are many variations of how ghosts are perceived, one thing remains the same, whether as a source of comfort or terror: They are with us, unseen. Sometimes they indicate their presence, sometimes they are mute, sometimes the manifestation is human in form, sometimes when something is simply moved—sometimes simply in lights with some form of a pattern—the variations seem endless. As long as mankind has been sentient, there has been a ghost story waiting to be told.

If you think about it, much of the religions and the philosophies that have shaped human culture have involved some form of spirit, whether visible or not. In some societies, ancestor worship has worked hand in hand with ghost myths and legends, and the same also goes for animism. In some societies, ghosts are also considered to be protectors of the living, their descendants. So ghosts tell us that there is a world beyond death and there is comfort in knowing that the living are protected by the dead.

That's not always the case, of course. Some societies consider ghosts to be evil and vindictive (although yet again, some societies don't). Some societies consider ghosts to be doomed to walk the earth for eternity, due to a curse of some kind or paying a penitence of some kind. Ghosts can be murder victims, also doomed to stay around in a particular place because they suffered trauma in their death and are unable to understand that they should leave (story idea: ghost therapists!). Along the same vein, ghosts may stay around because they were improperly buried (possibly because of their murder!). This is a common theme around the world, and not limited to ghosts (this pops up with vampires as well).

And of course, where these ghosts hang out is also of note. Haunted houses (or gardens or churches or what have you) often have regular manifestations at the same place and the same time. When these occurrences are recorded, it's also often the case that the spirits appear like a broken record; it's as though they're sleepwalking (ghostwalking?)(but of course, ghostwalkers are a whole different thing, as is the Ghost Who Walks, if you're a fan of the comic strip "The Phantom").

These manifestations aren't necessarily just human-like figures, although they are frequently described as such; in some cultures they can be animals or even insects. Sometimes there aren't any visual manifestations at all except as some physical phenomena (you're probably familiar with the legend of poltergeists), when solid objects are moved around or even thrown around (as a sign of displeasure). There are "ghost lights," balls of light sometimes caught on film (and usually dismissed as a trick or fault of photography, although there are no logical explanations for the layman). And ghost myths and astral projection occurrences have also been linked, in which the soul leaves the living body temporarily and travels, sometimes visible to the living. And of course, there's the theory of ghosts being psychic or electrical emissions.

Ghost myths and legends can be found all over the world, but what is remarkable is how many factors they have in common. But then, death happens everywhere along the Silk Road and beyond, so how cultures view ghosts should have many factors in common.

The Silk Road we'll be traveling goes all the way around the world, and we're going to start in the most unlikely of beginnings: Hollywood!

**Consider This:** Have you experienced some form of ghostly contact, and if so, what kind? What makes you think it was ghostly as opposed to technological? Or the neighbor kid being a brat?

Casper the Friendly Ghost. Note he has feet.

# Chapter 2
*Hooray for Ghostly Hollywood!*

As long as there have been dead people and live people to talk about them, ghosts have had a strong presence in storytelling, and Hollywood jumped on the bandwagon right from the beginning of the new technology. When we searched for "ghost" on IMDb (http://www.imdb.com), there were 2,999 results. That's a lot of films for 120 years or so. Evenly divided, that would be twenty films per year, and until the 1920s, the industry was shaky. We doubt many other subjects can claim such popularity.

There's a difference between folklore and movies. Many times, movies draw from lore but don't impinge on it; other times—not often, though—lore is actually changed by popular culture. As writers, we have to pay attention to the region and time frame because that will determine how we build the story world. Religion, whether real or made up by the author, is important because a majority of ghosts are spirits of the deceased, so there's the question of afterlife. The socio-economic circumstances of the main characters can have an effect on the story world as well. If we choose not to base our stories on actual lore and make up our own, which is what Jacquie usually does, it still behooves us to know what "rules" we're breaking.

For Hollywood, we actually need to start in Paris, because Georges Méliès wrote, directed, and starred in the first ghost movie, *Le cabinet de Méphistophélès* (The Devil's Laboratory), in 1897. This movie is very short, but the head of the ghost floats around the room—fodder for many, many movies to come. The next year, George Albert Smith from the UK directed *The Corsican Brothers*, based on the book by Alexander Dumas, where the ghost of one twin demonstrates to the other how he was killed.

Skip ahead a few years and jump over the pond. Now we're in Manhattan at the Edison Studios where the co-father of animation, J. Stuart Blackton, worked. These early years brought many new cinematography techniques and tricks, including stop/action. Using a combination of live action and drawings, Blackton directed and starred in *Hooligan Assists the Magician*, the first in a series of shorts where otherworldly spirits abound. The other co-father of animation would be Walter R. Booth in England, who in 1901 directed *Scrooge, or, Marley's Ghost,* written by Charles Dickens himself.

Why all this talk about animation? Because ghosts seldom show up at casting calls. Even if they did, they're hard to photograph. These original movie makers had to come up with visual methods by which to get around these problems and in so doing, built the foundation for all the special effects we see today.

Dickens shows up again when J. Searle Dawley directed *A Christmas Carol* for Edison Films in 1910. This film was a whopping ten minutes long, double that of the 1901 version—in a decade, the movie-making process expanded in technique and technology just as rapidly.

Probably the first really popular film featuring ghosts was *Topper*, made in 1938 and starring Cary Grant, Constance Bennett, and Roland Young. IMDb storyline:

The funloving Kerbys, stockholders in the bank of which henpecked, stuffy Cosmo Topper is president, drive recklessly once too often and become ghosts. In limbo because they've never done either good or bad deeds, they decide to try a good one: rehabilitating Topper. Lovely, flirtatious Marion takes a personal interest in the job. Will Topper survive the wrath of jealous ghost George? Will Mrs. Topper find that a scandalous husband isn't all bad?

The next year saw another stab at bringing *A Christmas Carol* to the big screen, this time as a full-length feature film of 69 minutes, starring Reginald Owen, Gene Lockhart, and Kathleen Lockhart. (A side note: Reginald Owen, who played Scrooge, also played Admiral Boom in *Mary Poppins*. He performed in more than 80 pictures.) This story was made into yet another movie titled *Scrooge* in 1951.

The year 1941 brought another ghost comedy, *The Ghost of St. Michael's*, starring Will Hay, Claude Hulbert, and Felix Aylmer. IMDb says:

Will Hay, back in his role as a hapless teacher, is hired by a grim school in remotest Scotland. The school soon starts to be haunted by a legendary ghost, whose spectral bagpipes signal the death of one of the staff. Hay, assisted by Claude Hulbert and Charles Hawtrey, has to unravel the mystery before he becomes the next victim.

In the same year, Abbott and Costello got in the act with *Hold That Ghost*. According to IMDb:

Two bumbling service station attendants are left as the sole beneficiaries in a gangster's will. Their trip to claim their fortune is sidetracked when they are stranded in a haunted house along with several other strangers.

*A Guy Named Joe*, made in 1943, might sound familiar to you:

Maj. Pete Sandidge is a very able pilot who seems to have a streak of luck as far as flying goes. World War II is raging and Pete has come out of it pretty well so far. He even has a beautiful girlfriend, Dorinda Durston, herself a qualified pilot who ferries aircraft to different bases. When Pete is killed however, he finds himself in heaven and learns that every pilot has a guardian angel. He returns to Earth where, unseen by anyone, he coaches a pilot-in-training, Ted Randall. Ted is a pretty good kid and is coming along nicely, but when he's shipped to New Guinea, he runs into Dorinda, who has remained faithful to her lost love. As Ted pursues her, Pete will have to decide what he wants to do about it.

Keep this one in mind because we'll see this plot again in about forty years.

Jump to 1945 for another comedic portrayal of ghosts. *Blithe Spirit* is a movie adapted from a play, where a couple is haunted by the husband's first (deceased) wife. It stars Rex Harrison, Constance Cummings, and Kay Hammond. Also in 1945, we were introduced to *Casper, the Friendly Ghost.* He starred in television shows and movies for 60 years—an enduring and endearing character. Trivia: Casper's last name is McFadden.

*The Ghost and Mrs. Muir* was released in 1947 starring Gene Tierney, Rex Harrison, and George Sanders. Lucy Muir is a widow who falls in love with a charming man, but is also in love with the ghost of the house's former owner. This movie was quite popular and spun off a television series (with a lot of changes) that aired from 1968 to 1970.

William Shakespeare's *Hamlet* was brought to the big screen in 1948, directed by Lawrence Olivier, who also played the role of Hamlet. We all know the story—Hamlet learns how the king (Hamlet's father) died by talking to his ghost and vows revenge. Olivier won Academy Awards for both Best Actor and Best Picture.

Let's skip a decade and go to a Vincent Price horror flick, *House on Haunted Hill,* released in 1959. There had been scary ghost movies all along but none were all that popular. This movie wasn't a box office smash, but did have a quality cast and crew. IMDb tells the story thus:

Eccentric millionaire Fredrick Loren and his fourth wife, Annabelle, have invited five people to the house on Haunted Hill for a "haunted house" party. Whoever stays in the house for one night will earn ten thousand dollars each. As the night progresses, all the guests are trapped inside the house with ghosts, murderers, and other terrors.

Contrast that with the horror/comedy of the same year, *The Headless Ghost,* where three college students have to help a ghost find his head, somewhere in Ambrose Castle.

Of course, during this time, television was airing *The Twilight Zone,* which was weird in many ways, and often had ghostly elements. Same with *The Alfred Hitchcock Hour.*

For an A-list horror flick, try *The Haunting,* released in 1963 starring Julie Harris, Claire Bloom, and Richard Johnson. IMDb explains the plot thus:

Dr. Markway, doing research to prove the existence of ghosts, investigates Hill House, a large, eerie mansion with a lurid history of violent death and insanity. With him are the skeptical young Luke, who stands to inherit the house, the mysterious and clairvoyant Theodora, and the insecure Eleanor, whose psychic abilities make her somehow attuned to whatever spirits inhabit the old mansion. As time goes by, it becomes obvious that they have gotten more than they bargained for as the ghostly presence in the house manifests itself in horrific and deadly ways.

Things lightened up considerably in 1966 with Don Knotts in *The Ghost and Mr. Chicken.* In 1968, Peter Ustinov, Dean Jones, and Suzanne Pleshette starred in *Blackbeard's Ghost.* This is a Disney comedy where the pirate/ghost, played by Ustinov, can't pass to the next world until he does a good deed. Ghosts were popular in the 1960s and often made an appearance on the wildly popular *Dark Shadows* television series as well as *Night Gallery.*

Woody Allen released *Play It Again, Sam* in 1972, where Allen's character, a mild-mannered film critic, receives dating advice from Humphrey Bogart's ghost.

In 1975, there was a TV series called *The Ghost Busters.* We'd never heard of this—it starred Forrest Tucker, Larry Storch, and Bob Burns. "Two guys and their pet gorilla hunt spooks." This doesn't have anything to do with the movies, but we thought it was interesting that the name had already been used. And of course, ghosts play a big part in many *Scooby Doo* episodes.

*The Sentinel* (1977) was a scary flick starring Chris Sarandon, Cristina Raines, and Martin Balsam, where a fashion model lived in an apartment that was the gate to Hell. This movie uses more of the traditional lore of ghosts being spirits who are the souls of dead people, stuck between Heaven and Hell.

James Brolin, Margot Kidder, and Rod Steiger tried to scare us out of our wits in 1979 with *The Amityville Horror*. A couple and their three kids move into a house that was the site of a murder, and evil ghosts haunt the place. This is based on a true story. It was a smash hit and is still popular on DVD today. And it was revisited in 2005. We can't seem to get enough of Amityville!

One of the scariest movies ever was based a Stephen King story, *The Shining*, released in 1980 and starred Jack Nicholson (of course) and Shelley Duvall. Remember REDRUM? Yikes! Here's the IMDb summary:
Jack Torrance gets a job as the custodian of the Overlook Hotel, in the mountains of Colorado. The place is closed down during winter, and Torrance and his family will be the only occupants of the hotel for a long while. When the snowstorms block the Torrance family in the hotel, Jack's son Danny, who has some clairvoyance and telepathy powers, discovers that the hotel is haunted and that the spirits are slowly driving Jack crazy. When Jack meets the ghost of Mr. Grady, the former custodian of the hotel who murdered his wife and his two daughters, things begin to get really nasty.

If you weren't scared enough, two years later Steven Spielberg brought us *The Poltergeist,* starring Craig T. Nelson, JoBeth Williams, and Beatrice Straight. Ghosts move into the family home. At first they seem harmless, but then get nasty and kidnap the youngest daughter. *Poltergeist II: The Other Side* was released in 1986.

Who you gonna call??? Probably the most popular

ghost movie ever was released in 1984. Probably every one of us has seen it—*Ghostbusters!* It starred Dan Aykroyd and Harold Ramis, who also co-wrote it. IMDb says Rick Moranis was also a writer, uncredited. Also starring was Bill Murray, Sigourney Weaver, and Annie Potts. Lots of A-listers had cameos as well. IMDb explains the plot:

Three oddball scientists get kicked out of their cushy positions at a university in New York City where they studied the occult. They decide to set up shop in an old firehouse and become Ghostbusters, trapping pesky ghosts, spirits, haunts, and poltergeists for money. They wisecrack their way through the city, and stumble upon a gateway to another dimension, one that will release untold evil upon the city. The Ghostbusters must save the Big Apple.

There was a *Ghostbusters* television series spinoff, and then the second movie, innovatively titled *Ghostbusters II*, was released in 1989. The latest in the series was released in 2016, but with the twist of the Ghostbusters all being female and defending Boston instead of New York.

One of our favorite films is *Beetlejuice*, released in 1988, starring Michael Keaton, Geena Davis, and Alec Baldwin. A married couple are proud of their house, but they happen to be dead. When a family moves in, the two ghosts try their best to get the family to leave, and enlist the aid of Beetlejuice to help. What a fun movie, and who can forget the "Banana Boat Song" scene? This movie spun off a television series of the same title.

From comedy we head to sentimental romance—it's Spielberg's remake of *A Guy Named Joe*, mentioned earlier. This film's title is *Always* and starred Richard Dreyfuss, Holly Hunter, and John Goodman, released in 1989. The plot's pretty much the same except instead of fighter pilots, it's about firefighter pilots and is filmed in the beautiful Kootenai National Forest. Your heart melts when they dance to "Smoke Gets in Your Eyes." This film wasn't that well received, but we think it's one of Spielberg's best.

And speaking of romance, one of the most romantic ghost movies was released in 1990. *Ghost* starred Patrick Swayze, Demi Moore, and Whoopi Goldberg. The pottery wheel scene is a classic. Here's the IMDb summary:

Sam and Molly are a very happy couple and deeply in love. Walking back to their new apartment after a night out at the theater, they encounter a thief in a dark alley, and Sam is murdered. He finds himself trapped as a ghost and realizes that his death was no accident. He must warn Molly about the danger that she is in. But as a ghost he cannot be seen or heard by the living, and so he tries to communicate with Molly through Oda Mae Brown, a psychic who didn't even realize that her powers were real.

We're not sure if *Candyman* is a ghost movie or not. Jacquie's daughter saw it and all the people in the theater behind her ended up with popcorn in their hair when she was so startled that somehow the carton jumped out of her hands and emptied itself. She was so scared she couldn't remember, but the character sounds like a ghost to us—he was murdered and comes back when his name is repeated five times. This film was released in 1992.

That same year, the Muppets reprised Charles Dickens's story in *The Muppet Christmas Carol.* Michael Caine plays Scrooge in this one. Someone remakes this story every few years—it's a beloved story, it screens well, and has all the elements of a hit with multi-dimensional characters and a solid plot. And ghost stories at Christmas sell well.

*Casper* made another appearance in 1995, the movie bearing his name. This film stars everyone from Mr. Rogers to Eric Idle. It's a fun one, about an heiress who inherits a haunted mansion.

Peter Jackson brought us *The Frighteners* in 1996 starring Michael J. Fox, Trini Alvarado, and Peter Dobson. It's a comedy/horror flick. IMDb plot summary goes like this:

After a car accident in which his wife, Debra, was killed and he was injured, Frank Bannister develops psychic abilities allowing him to see, hear, and communicate with ghosts. He gives up his job as an architect and puts these skills to use by befriending a few ghosts and getting them to haunt houses in the area to drum up work for his ghostbusting business; Frank proceeds to "exorcise" the houses for a fee. But when he discovers that an entity resembling the Grim Reaper is killing people, marking numbers on their forehead beforehand, Frank tries to help the people whom the Reaper is after!

In 1997, we had *Spawn*, based on the comic book. The main character isn't billed as a ghost but he's dead and comes back to earth to see his wife, so we're including it. The IMDb summary goes like this:

An assassin named Al Simmons is double-crossed and murdered by his evil boss, Jason Wynn. Al makes a deal with the devil and returns to earth as Spawn to see his wife. He is ordered by the devil's minion, The Clown, to kill Wynn. Wynn has made a deal with the clown too and is supposed to destroy the world with a deadly virus that will help start Armageddon and allow Hell to attack Heaven. Spawn must choose between good and evil.

A little boy claims to see ghosts in *The Sixth Sense* with Bruce Willis and Haley Joel Osment, released in 1999.

Willis plays child psychiatrist Malcolm Crowe, who's confronted and shot one night by a former patient, who then kills himself. After several months of recovery, Crowe is hired to treat Cole Sear, a boy who has similar issues. Crowe hopes to help Cole, but has serious doubts when Cole claims to see ghosts who don't know they're dead.

Let's talk Johnny Depp!  The year 1999 also brought us Tim Burton's *The Legend of Sleepy Hollow* starring Johnny Depp, Christina Ricci, and Miranda Richardson, adapted from the story by Washington Irving.  All sorts of spooky things terrorized the people of Sleepy Hollow, but of course the headless horseman was the scariest.  IMDb says:

The curse of the headless horseman is the legacy of the small town of Sleepy Hollow. Spearheaded by the eager Constable Ichabod Crane and his new world ways into the quagmire of secrets and murder, secrets once laid to rest, best forgotten and now reawakened, and he too, holding a dark secret of a past once gone.

This story was revisited almost a decade and a half later.

In 2000, Michelle Pfeiffer starred in *What Lies Beneath*, where a retired concert cellist hears ghostly voices and sees a young girl's face on the surface of a lake.  Also that year, in light of all the teenage horror cash cows, Dimension Films released *Scary Movie*.  That one didn't have ghosts in it, but in 2001 they released *Scary Movie 2,* and it did.

Here's a genuine ghost movie: *Thir13en Ghosts.* The IMDB summary goes like this:

When Cyrus Kriticos, a very rich collector of unique things, dies, he leaves it all to his nephew and his family— including his house, his fortune, and his malicious collection of ghosts!

*Harry Potter and the Sorcerer's Stone* featured Lord Draben, the Ghost of the Cavalier (one of the better characters!), played by Paul Marc Davis. There are also house ghosts, and in some of the other Harry Potter movies, we have Moaning Myrtle. Ghosts are generally not scary in the Harry Potter franchise.

The years 2001–2003 brought us the *Lord of the Rings* trilogy, and the first *Pirates of the Caribbean*. Neither of these are exactly ghost movies, but both have elements of the undead in a more ghostly manner than in a vampirish manner. Then again, if you have Viggo Mortensen *and* Johnny Depp, who cares.

The TV show *Supernatural* first aired in 2005. Brothers Sam and Dean Winchester hunt all sorts of paranormal entities, ghosts being prime game. And in 2007, back to horror, we have *Dead Silence*. The plot, according to IMDB: "A widower returns to his hometown to search for answers to his wife's murder, which may be linked to the ghost of a murdered ventriloquist." We also had *Ghost Rider* starring Nicolas Cage, based on the comic book. The only legit ghost was the Caretaker, Sam Elliott. Ah, but what a ghost!

A comedy romance, *Ghost Town*, was released in 2008 starring Greg Kinnear, Jordan Carlos, and Ricky Gervais. "Bertram Pincus is a man whose people skills leave much to be desired. When Pincus dies unexpectedly but is miraculously revived after seven minutes, he wakes up to discover that he now has the annoying ability to see ghosts." (Also from IMDb.) The UK television show *Being Human* aired that year also. It featured a werewolf, a vampire, and a ghost. There is also an American version.

Ghosts continued to be popular in 2012 when *The Woman in Black* was released starring Emma Shorey, Daniel Radcliffe, and Ciarán Hinds. According to IMDb: "A young lawyer travels to a remote village where he discovers the vengeful ghost of a scorned woman is terrorizing the locals."

Sleepy Hollow popped up again in 2013, with the original story by Washington Irving very loosely adapted and taken for another turn on TV. In this version Sleepy Hollow is a much bigger town, Ichabod Crane a British soldier in the American Revolution turned a spy for the Americans, asleep for more than 200 years come awake in present day, and now fighting the Four Horsemen of the Apocalypse. Ghosts are around, but there's a lot more to it.

Most recently, and speaking of Winchester, there's the movie *Winchester* (2018), a horror movie about the famous house in San Jose, California, starring Helen Mirren.

There are many ghost movies—lots not included here, and if you add in television, there are a jillion more. Ghosts actually are more popular on TV and in books. Cartoons, comics, dramas, and even soap operas have ghost characters. They're also popular in video games, which we're not covering at all, but show you the broad appeal of ghosts as characters. All for another day (and book)!

It's impossible to discuss all the movies and television programs that deal with ghosts, so this lesson only hits on the bare minimum highlights. Did we forget something big? What's your favorite ghost movie or program?

**Consider This:** Do you find ghost stories in Hollywood to be fun, frightening, or infuriating and why?

Symbol of Great Spirit, principal deity of some Native American peoples.

# Chapter 3
*Ghosts in the Americas*

Whether an apparition is a ghost, faery, angel, or demon often depends on who's relating the myth and where it's set. All four of these entities are often identified as the souls of the dead who are between realms, whether Valhalla, Hades, Tuonela, the Garden of the Gods, Heaven, or any of the other terms used for where we spend the afterlife.

A good general article examining the role of ghosts in cultures is "The Folklore of Ghosts and Hauntings" by Brian Haughton. He points out the difference between a ghost and a haunting—a ghost is an apparition, smell, sound, or something we sense. A haunting is a place where ghosts hang out.

We've looked at a number of Hollywood films and seen the moviemakers' interpretations, so let's take a look at the ghost lore in the Americas. One thing is abundantly clear: Americans love their ghosts, whether spooky, woeful, educational, ornery, or funny. The Internet is loaded with sites about ghosts and ghost lore, and a gajillion books have been written on the subject. We have ghost towns, ghost trains, and ghost ships. We have haunted houses, hotels, mines, shopping malls, and even ghosts in the White House. Jacquie's grandsons even swear there's a ghost in her garage!

We'll look at the ghosts of Americans of European descent in a bit, but first, let's take a peek at the ghosts of those who already lived here.

There's the Cheyenne story of the ghost with two faces, like the Roman god Janus, one forward, one backward. This ghost decides to marry one day and courts a live maiden, but when she rejects him—the fact that he's a ghost, and that he's got two faces apparently a deal-breaker—the maiden's father has to trick the ghost into a game of find-the-shell. (The version of the story we found didn't use "shells," but it's a reference more readers would be familiar with.) The father, it turns out, is the best shell-game player in the world, and no matter how many games the ghost plays with the father, the ghost always loses. So the ghost has to supply the maiden's family with plentiful game and step away from his courtship of the maiden. We're not sure what the moral of the story is, but it did point out that Cheyenne ghosts keep up their part of a deal.

Most Native American ghosts are benevolent, but nasty apparitions exist as well. In the Northeast, the Abenaki, Penobscot, Maliseet, and Passamaquoddy have the ghost of the Swamp Woman, who lives in the swamps and wails a mournful song. Some say she lures children to the swamp so she can eat them, but others claim she's mourning the loss of her own child. Either way, parents warn their children about her and she serves as a good deterrent for keeping children from going too close to the dangerous swamp. There's a similar legend in the Central American region.

Then there's the White Stallion Ghost. This is in the

Cree culture. A tribal leader was abusive to his wives and those less fortunate. In lean times, he profited by trading food for poorer people's valuables instead of helping one and all. No one liked him and he didn't like them either. What he adored was his horses—but only the young and beautiful. One day, he checked his herd and he found a scruffy white stallion. The man beat the stallion and broke his legs, leaving him to die. When the man went out to check his herd the next day, his herd was gone, and he found only a beautiful white stallion—a ghost. The ghost horse told the man if he wanted his herd, he'd have to walk two days north. Once the man did that, the horse told him he'd have to walk two days east. And to this day, the man has never again slept in his own lodge or been able to claim a single horse.

Native American lore nearly always has several lessons within one story. The Blackfoot (Piegans) have an interesting Ghost Camp story about a man who couldn't live without his late wife, in an echo of the Orpheus and Eurydice story.

A brief version: Overcome with grief, the man sets out to find his wife in the spirit world. He's invited to a camp—a tribe of ghosts. His wife is there and he's given a Worm Pipe and medicine with instructions for its use as well as how to return to his own world. He follows these difficult instructions, returns to camp with his wife, who has now come back to physical life.

According to the Legends of America website: "That is how the people came to possess the Worm Pipe. That pipe belongs to the band of Piegans known as the Worm People.

"Not long after this, once in the night, this man told his

wife to do something, and when she did not begin at once he picked up a brand from the fire and raised it—not that he intended to strike her with it, but he made as if he would—when all at once she vanished and was never seen again."

The lessons are to always follow instructions exactly or reap the consequences; and that it's never acceptable to raise a hand to your wife, whether you intend to strike her or not.

We could go on and on—there are hundreds of wonderful Native American ghost stories from all peoples covering every square inch of North America. You'll find lots of ghost stories from various Native American peoples here: http://www.native-languages.org/legends-ghost.htm

Everyone in America seems to have a ghost or a ghost story. No matter where you go, there's a ghost tour or at least some juicy ghost stories. We'll list a few, but wherever you set your book, there'll be a local ghost legend, we can guarantee it. We do love our ghosts.

Jacquie has a ghost character in her *Honey Beaulieu – Man Hunter* western series named Roscoe, who rides Luther, a three-legged ghost horse. Roscoe died when his girlfriend's jealous boyfriend shot him. Luther died later, and the two of them were reunited in the afterlife. Roscoe is a fun character because he shows up at inopportune times and his advice to Honey Beaulieu as she's learning to be a bounty hunter isn't always the best—but he has good intentions. Overall, it's a 50/50 shot whether he helps or hinders Honey in her pursuits.

*An Indian Princess at Pike Place Market*
Long before there was a Seattle as we know it today, when the Duwamish Natives signed the Treaty of Point Elliott, all the Indians were supposed to move out of the area. But Kikisoblu, daughter of Chief Seattle (Si'ahl or Sealth), better known to whites as Princess Angeline, stayed in her cabin on the Seattle waterfront. She lived there for forty more years until her death.

A decade later, in 1911, Pike Place Market was built where her cabin had been. And apparently she wasn't ready to leave yet, because even today, people claim to see Princess Angeline wandering about the market. There's nothing to show where she lived right now, so you have to do some hunting to find the spot.

*A Ghost Ship in Wyoming?*
Yep, that's right. The Platte River in southeast Wyoming is home to a very scary, and bizarre, ghost ship. Three times it's been seen and all three times the person witnessed the death of a loved one on the ship—and yes, all three times the loved one died later that very day. You can read all about it at Tom Rizzo's blog, at tomrizzo.com.

*The HMS Queen Mary*
Lots of ghosts have been reported to live in the *HMS Queen Mary*, currently docked in Long Beach, California. A man named John Henry worked in the engine room and was killed in a fire. Engine Room 13's door is reportedly often hot to the touch, and smoke wisps around it occasionally. Many passersby have heard knocking as if someone were trying to get out. Then there are the three female ghosts seen around the pool—one little girl and two women.

From the website yourghoststories.com: "The in-house

psychic, Peter James, claims that he has communicated with over 150 separate ghosts on the ship. Peter gives bi-monthly ghost tours of the ship and claims to have made numerous contact[s] with various ghosts, including a few mentioned above. From the sheer number and type of deaths that occurred, it seems plausible."

*Winchester Mystery House*
While we're in California, we might as well stop by one of the most famous haunted mansions in America, the Winchester Mystery House. Heiress Sarah Winchester felt that the ghosts and spirits of those killed with Winchester firearms needed to be appeased. She felt that they needed a nice comfy place to live, and all the amenities thereof. *But* they also followed her.  As a result, construction continued day and night so the spirits knew she was always improving their environs, building elaborate mazes, doors, and stairways that went nowhere, secret rooms, and a confusing floor plan (or unplan, as the case may be).

Even Henry Houdini went to the Winchester House to visit the spirits. In 2018, the movie *Winchester*, written and directed by the Spierig brothers and starring Helen Mirren, was released to relatively tepid reviews.

*Galveston, Texas*
The city of Galveston has seen a lot of tragedy—the hurricane of 1900 killed a good quarter of the inhabitants. Most buildings that survived have hosted ghostly apparitions, and currently there are several ghost tours offered.  One such place is the Ashton Villa Mansion, built by James Brown before the Civil War.  The mansion was used as a hospital, and many died there.  Because it was built with brick and cast iron, it survived the hurricane, and so did the ghosts of the soldiers.

But the predominant ghost is Bettie, the owner's daughter, mistress of the house after his death in 1895. Her ghost is still there today, mostly standing at the top of the stairs or in her dayroom—the only room where she could relax without her stays.

*New Orleans*
The most renowned ghost in residence in this city of ghosts has to be Voodoo Queen Marie Catherine Laveau, buried in St. Louis Cemetery No. 1. Her legacy was compounded by her daughter, also named Marie, and encrypted in the same cemetery. Paranormal seekers have witnessed both women hanging out there.

The first Marie was born in 1801. Both parents were free, as was she. Her heritage consisted of Native American, African, and French descent. Marie held various jobs throughout her life, including liquor importer, matchmaker at the famed Placage Balls, and hairdresser to wealthy white matrons, as well as, you know, Voodoo Queen. She died in 1881, and is said to still roam St. Louis Cemetery No. 1.

In New Orleans, nearly every building that has been in existence over a hundred years has its own resident ghost. There's the Creole woman named Mam at the Bourbon Club. Pierre Antoine Lepardi Jourdan still roams Muriel's restaurant, so you can get a bite to eat *and* see a ghost while you're at it. Visit the Pharmacy Museum and you might run into some of the victims of Dr. Joseph Dupas who died in 1867. Or you can go to the Myrtles Plantation where you might see Chloe, who's said to have poisoned her children after their father ended their affair—for which she was subsequently hanged. People have reported seeing many other ghosts there as well.

The oldest ghost haunt known has to be Lafitte's Blacksmith Shop, now a bar. It's said that Jean Lafitte himself is still there, guarding the treasure hidden in the fireplace grate. The most gruesome is the LaLaurie Mansion, where Madame LaLaurie tortured slaves to their deaths. And one of the nicest ghosts is Friar Antonio de Sedella, also known as Pere Antoine, pastor of the St. Louis Church, where people report seeing his spirit to this day.

Many, many other ghosts call New Orleans home, a veritable cornucopia of spirits for paranormal writers.
http://www.frenchquarter.com/new-orleans-ghosts/
https://www.whereyat.com/new-orleans-most-famous-ghosts

*The White House*
Lots of ghosts have been seen and sensed in the White House by staff, Presidents, and first ladies. Among the White House specters is apparently Abigail Adams. The house was still under construction when John Adams was President, but she and John moved in nonetheless and Abigail worked hard to create a Presidential home. Another spirit is said to be of David Burns, the landowner who sold the acreage to the government. The two most frequently seen ghosts are Abraham Lincoln and Andrew Jackson.

George W. Bush has a page about ghosts on his archives website, at
http://georgewbush-whitehouse.archives.gov.

*Civil War Ghosts*
Many of the famous Civil War battlegrounds are said to harbor ghosts. There's a website that talks about the ghosts

at Gettysburg:
http://communities.washingtontimes.com/neighborhood/
civil-war/2012/oct/28/civil-war-ghosts-still-haunt-
gettysburg-and-antiet/

Take a look at this YouTube video. They claim it's Mrs. Henry and you can see her at 15 seconds and 21 seconds.
http://youtu.be/G27tgEiUE2o

"My family and I were on vacation in DC and we went to the Manassas battlefield. We videotaped there, and later that day we were watching the tape and we noticed the woman dressed in white walking along the fenceline. There were no reenactments going on that day, and we didn't see her there. If you look to the left of the house, you will see a small black fence with a marker that encloses the graves of Mrs. Henry, her daughter, and her son. The ghost is walking away from the graves to just an open field. We are convinced that this was a paranormal experience."

Then there's the white lady myth—that is, the story of a woman dressed in a white shroud who appears out of nowhere and often seems to warn of an impending danger, only to disappear afterward—can be found all over the world, including Texas, where, we discovered, there is a variation involving the lady wearing white Neiman-Marcus clothing. More on mysterious white ladies in our chapter about Pacific Rim ghosts.

*Heading South Beyond The Border*
Ghosts are an embedded part of Mexican culture, stemming from the Mayan and Aztec civilizations that were around long before the Spanish invasion. The Day of the Dead celebration observed now includes pre-Columbian beliefs imbued with later Christian elements, and Mexican popular

media includes many stories involving ghosts.

*La Llorona*
In the Honduras, the story goes that a woman named Maria fell madly in love with a man. He wanted her but not her children, so she drowned them. But it was all for naught because he refused to be with a woman who'd do such a thing. When she died, the gates of heaven were closed to her and she became the ghost La Llorona. She haunts the lakes and rivers of Central America, wailing for her children. In some versions of the legends, she actually takes children and drowns them. This has echoes of the Swamp Woman story from the Native Americans, and when we get to Europe, we'll see variations of this same story. (This particular legend was used in an episode of the TV show *Grimm*.)

*Gaucho Gil*
Once we go south, we encounter some interesting spirit variations, one of which is Gaucho Gil, Argentina's own ghostly Robin Hood who robbed from the rich and gave to the poor.

*Saltpeter Ghosts*
In Chile, in an abandoned saltpeter mine called Humberstone (named after a guy from England who founded the Peru Nitrate Company), live many ghosts. One is apparently the ghost of a woman who was killed by a train. Her son was playing on the tracks and she saved him, but the train ran over her. She haunts the train station still. Other Humberstone ghosts are unidentified, but they're plentiful.

Then there's the jima out of the Amazon River, scary spirits that grab the living with cold hands laced with poison and tear the victim's soul out of the body.

This is just a sampling of the diverse collection of ghosts in the Americas.  Do you have a favorite ghost story from the Americas?  Please share!

**Consider This:** Do you have a favorite ghost story? Why is it your favorite?

The concept of a haunted house seems to be pretty much everywhere.

# Chapter 4
*Ghosts Across Northern Europe
and the British Isles*

We bid farewell to the Americas and then it's just a hop skip and a jump across the Atlantic before we arrive at what we refer to the Old World. It's a big place, Europe is, but much of its ghost lore have a lot in common with each other, and it's easier to compare and contrast all in a big lesson. So get set to consider a lot of ghost stories, folks, because the Old World—Europe, both Eastern and Western, the Nordic countries, and parts south from there—has a goodly share of them.

For the most part, the ghosts that first come to mind when we use that word are the ones we've read about and heard about from the various cultures of Europe, most notably German and Scandinavia. The Grimm brothers did an excellent job of wandering from village to village gathering folktales, and in doing so, they also noted similarities and differences between versions of the same story. We found out how much we really have in common throughout Europe.

Let's begin up in the northern climes and work our way down. Starting with ghosts in the Nordic countries which, unlike those in some other cultures (for example, see

Greeks and Romans), look like their living brethren and are even occasionally confused with them. They are often distinguished by odd behavior, an inability to speak, or a sudden appearance and disappearance.

Like other countries both close by and far away, there are ghosts that haunt and ghosts that grieve and ghosts that avenge. In the Scandinavian countries, there's the *myling*, the spirit of a child left to die in the wilderness, and the *mara*, a malevolent ghost that causes nightmares and sleep paralysis. You've probably heard of the *will o' the wisp*—who hasn't?—and up north, they're said to be the ghosts of those who drowned in lakes. They can be hostile or helpful, because there are stories in which they lead a living being who's lost back to their home but other stories in which they lure the lost to their doom in the water.

Water is a recurrent theme here in the Nordic countries. The *draugr* is the ghost of a man who drowned out in the open sea. He appears as a corpse or in skeletal form covered in seaweed and screams a blood-curdling cry, and he shows up at night during storms at sea, drowning sailors and fishermen and sinking their vessels. If the seafarers spot him, they know he's there to drown them, so they must race to land if possible to thwart him.

There are land versions, too, but these ghosts live in graves and possess the living. Land draugs are noted to hoard treasure, are very strong, and are known to shapeshift (a skinned bull, a horse with a broken back, and a cat are three common shifts). These draugs rise from their graves as smoke and kill humans who would disturb their sleep or trespass the graveyard by eating them, crushing them (they can also change size), and drinking their blood. Understandably, animals don't like being around an area known to have draugs. Either land or sea, draugs are thought to have been more or less evil during their lives, and continue their ways afterward.

Then there's the *gjenganger*, the ghost of someone who was also violent or bloodthirsty in life, who continues to threaten and harass even after death.

Then there are Viking ghosts. Not just Scandinavian, not just Norse, but Viking ghosts! Well, not necessarily ghosts per se. Apparently the culture had vivid and colorful stories about Vikings' exploits about their battles and how they got to be dead and what they did afterward. But Viking shades just continue to exist in their own graves (spending most of their time singing, according to one source) and pop out once in a while to cause problems among the living. Instead of ghosts, the Vikings were more likely to believe they were possessed by evil spirits, according to Scandinavian native and author Åsa Maria Bradley.

But later on, after the Vikings had become part of history, there were Swedish ghosts. (The Swedish word for "ghost" is *spöke*, from the Old German word "spook." Ain't language wonderful?) The local lore said that Scandinavian ghosts were only allowed to move around between midnight and dawn. If a ghost were caught out of its grave at sunrise, they froze and became invisible until the sun went down again. If a living person brushed up against one of these frozen ghosts, the person would be struck by an unexplainable illness or pain.

Åsa Maria Bradley also mentions that one of the most famous haunts in Sweden is Ängsö Castle, dating from the 1100s. One of the best-known strange tales is about the devil's chain of Ängsö. In the story, if a certain golden chain, won by the lord of the castle in an ill-advised and odd game of dice in the middle of the night with a mysterious stranger (thought to be the devil), ever leaves the premises, unexplainable fires break out. Only the lord may wear it, to boot. The chain and dice are on display at the castle; the chain is estimated to be five feet long and created in a method that would have been difficult if not impossible back then, with equally odd markings on it.

But the ghost best associated with this castle is named Britta Bååt. Every night at a specific time, according to the legend, she makes her way through the castle and into a ballroom. According to the legend, she lived there during the 1500s and was not the nicest person around, and managed to drive two husbands into early graves. One Christmas Eve, she hurried to the local church for midnight mass when she saw a light shining there, but when she opened the door, it turned out to be a service made up of skeletons.

She was attacked by the spirits of her husbands, one of whom threw a sword at her (but missed) and the other threw a large rock, which also missed her. But the shock of being (finally) attacked by her late husbands was too much, and she died three days later. The sword and the stone (referred to as the "blood stone") with which she was attacked are walled up in the churchyard wall.

Then there are the *dísir*, female ghosts connected to a given family. (Family ghosts, usually used as housekeepers, are pretty common all around the world; there will be other examples throughout our journey.) The servants of the goddess Freyja, the disir are protective of their families and benevolent toward them, visiting homes with newborn babies to bring good luck. And if there are any enemies of the household planning death, doom, and destruction, well, good luck, because disir don't take kindly to that.

A small step over geographically but very different from the Scandinavian culture you know (but still part of the Nordic region) is Finland. Finnish mythology is distinctively different from the Scandinavians, stunningly so (don't get us started on the Finnish creation myth!). Many Finnish myths are shared with its neighbors in the nearby Baltic states (but not Scandinavian). Ghosts don't seem to take center stage as they often do in other cultures nearby, but the myths are notable nonetheless.

Finnish myths start off with that creation myth (broken eggshells!) and go on with Lintukoto, the home of the birds (and meaning "paradise"), where they lived during the inhospitable winters. The Milky Way is referred to as "Linnunrata," the path of the birds, because Finnish myths had the birds following the path that the Milky Way carved to and from Finland.

Birds are big in Finnish cultural myths. Birds—like storks, say—brought human souls to birth and took the souls away at death. The bird taking the soul away from life, referred to as the "soul bird," protected it from getting lost among the land of dreams on the way to Tuonela, the Finnish land of the dead.

Tuonela, like the Hades of Greek myth, is the underground home of the dead, not split off into good or indifferent like the Greeks. Tuonela is described as dark and lifeless (which make sense), where the dead remain asleep. For the living to travel there to ask for advice involved putting oneself into a trance and crossing the river of Tuonela. But first the traveler had to persuade the ferryman that he had a good reason to do so. On occasion in Finnish myth, the traveler would have to trick the guards at the land of the dead and the ferryman into thinking he was indeed dead for him to get in.

The river to cross into the land of the dead is a common theme around the world. We'll see it when we get to the Middle East and the river Jordan, and when we get to Japan and the river Sanzu.

The most famous ghost story from the Finns involves Olavinlinna, also known as St. Olaf's Castle, a fortress from the medieval period, with the love story of the Finnish maiden. The daughter of the castle's lord fell in love with a Russian soldier (it is important to note that the Finns and the Russians were constantly at war with each other during this period). The soldier betrayed her, but was killed when he let his forces in to take over the garrison. For her treasonous act, the maiden was buried alive in the courtyard, with a rowan tree growing where she was buried. Is the story based on fact? There's no tree there now, but the story persists, and there are tales of the lovelorn maiden being sighted from time to time.

As we travel east and south, we hop over to the Baltic states, and Russia, all of which have their own ghost stories. The legends of Tallinn give a hint of what can be found in the way of ghosts waiting to be discovered in this area. The ghost stories we see in this region can be as intertwined as Asian tales can be with a similar theme.

Starting with Estonia, there's a story about a house haunted by a jeweler, a goldsmith who was known as the Black Baron. With echoes of the Swedish story of Ängsö Castle and the golden chain known as the devil's chain, the jeweler sold his goods to any in town who could afford his prices. But it was well-known that he practiced black magic and all he created was cursed, with those who wore his pieces dying of mysterious circumstances soon thereafter. So don't try on any jewelry you just find lying around. You really don't know where it's been.

Tallinn, the capital of Estonia, has a famous ghost story known as the devil's wedding. Is it really a ghost story? Depends on your interpretation. In any case, there is a particular house that has a window bricked up on the top floor, with a picture of curtains painted there to be seen from the street. This house is where the landlord was approached by a man who offered a great deal of money to rent the top-floor apartment for an evening, ostensibly for a party—but he required absolute privacy. During the party, those beneath heard a racket, as if dozens of guests were running up and down the stairs. But at 1 a.m. sharp, the noise stopped dead. A servant who had been peering through the keyhole was found gravely ill, and before he died, he claimed that the devil himself had been having a wedding party!

Then from the website Atlas Obscura, there's a story about an abandoned graveyard in a small parish in Latvia. There you'll find an etched stone and the rusting, discarded pieces of a metal cross. The story behind the stone involves a dead child (neither boy nor girl, the legend goes), who was buried in the graveyard. The child's spirit could not be laid to rest, however, because the townsfolk soon found themselves unable to sleep with a constant scream emanating from the graveyard. A stone was ordered etched, with an accompanying cross to be placed on the child's grave. But the scream continued. Only after thirteen crosses had been etched on the stone did the noise finally stop. The article notes that the Baltic states were among the last European regions to undergo Christianization, and so local myths and paganism survived until the 18th century or so.

Then from Lithuania, another old country in the region, comes another distinct set of beliefs and folklore, including its view on the dead well-documented by its scholars (its main university is well over 400 years old). Its belief system echoes much of the region, with its own specific twist, the concept of death personified as the goddess Giltiné. She is described as a skeleton wrapped in a white cloak and carrying a scythe. She is also a killer, stinging her victims with a long tongue (the name is derived from the verb meaning to sting), by strangling, or with the scythe. She can also be glimpsed by the very sick or dying. Then there are the three white maidens who were reported to come to claim a life, while there was also a goddess of the plague (this most often during the plague period in the early 18th century, where it was estimated that the country lost a third of its population).

Russian folk tales often connect vampires and ghosts, something we'll see later in the Romanian tales (you remember Romania, don't you? Of course you do). But here's a Russian tale about a lazy girl that is reminiscent of the Britta Bååt story from Sweden. This girl preferred to spend her time gossiping and avoiding her work. She decided to invite the other girls in her village to a spinning party, promising to feed them, so that they would do her spinning for her. It worked, they did, and she fed them, as promised. At one point, she takes the dare of stealing an icon from the local church. She accepts the dare, with the proviso that the others must spin an extra amount for her.

She steals the icon and brings it back to the others. But

what to do with it, now that it was past midnight? The lazy girl decides to take the picture back, because she has also boasted that she is brave. So she takes it back—and on her way back from replacing the picture, she sees a corpse in a white shroud sitting in the graveyard. The foolish, foolish girl steals the shroud.

The girl displays the shroud she's stolen to the other girls, who are less impressed. But the corpse knocks at the window after they've gone to sleep, asking for its shroud back.

The other girls are understandably terrified. But the lazy girl (or perhaps we should just refer to her as foolish) bundles up the shroud, opens the window, and tosses it at the corpse. But the corpse says no, it has to be put back to the place from which it had been stolen. The foolish girl opts not to. The following night, the corpse comes again, asking for its shroud. The parents of the girl tries to give it to him, but again, the corpse insists it must be replaced whence it had been stolen. The following morning, the local priest is called in on the situation, and he suggests the lazy, foolish girl come to church the next day. She does—and when the service begins, a whirlwind so strong it knocks down the congregation comes into the church and grabs the girl, leaving no trace of her but strands of her dark hair.

*Working Our Way Through Europe, We Reach...*
Hey, we're in Germany! Or the region of Germany, since there are many cultures, many peoples, that make up the area. Wikipedia notes that German folklore shares a great deal with Scandinavian folklore and English folklore, both of which pop media are very familiar with. And of course, those Grimm brothers, those gatherers of folktales, noted how so much of it sounded familiar, with variations found

in widespread areas. (Even some of American storyteller Washington Irving's stories were based on German folktales.)

Now, German ghosts are very familiar to Americans. There's the *poltergeist*, literally "noisy ghost" in German, where an uneasy spirit moves things and throws things, which has been the basis for many a scary story (and quite a few frauds). There's the *revenant*, a term used throughout Europe, not just for ghosts but for vampires as well. Revenants rise from their graves and are known to do so to harass the living (once more) and avenge their deaths.

Then there is the *dybbuk* of Yiddish folklore, a malevolent ghost with the ability to possess the living. Jewish folklore has vivid stories about ghosts. In the Talmud there is a reference to a ghost (known as a *shade*), a being that lacks solid matter, and since it has no mass, it has the ability to transport from one place to another.

Ghosts in Europe from the medieval period forward were divided into the souls of the dead and demons. The former rose from their graves with a specific purpose—for revenge, say—while the latter only made themselves known for evil deeds. It was in this period during which ghosts became actively evil. Ghosts from this era in Europe were sometimes described as being more solid, actually challenging and battling living opponents until a priest could subdue them (these were of the demonic variety). Most of the ghosts reported were (for whatever reason) male.

It's also about this period that ghost reports were of not individuals, but of entire armies, battling in the forest, or at the remains of Iron Age forts (circa 800 BC to 50 AD).

There were even reports of knights challenged to a battle by ghost knights. During this period, ghosts were far more likely to settle in and make themselves comfortable, sticking around for longer periods and reporting from the beyond (and apparently complaining about purgatory, in one French case in 1211), getting involved in detailed discussions about theology. But since in one case the ghost spoke through his very much alive cousin, one has to wonder if the cousin wasn't being used as a vessel at all. This question arises because the ghost apparently also reported that God was happy about the ongoing Crusade at the time.

The comfort with ghosts existing alongside the living went on through the years. Shakespeare's Hamlet and his conversation with his father's ghost is a fine example of this. Even a few centuries later, English literature had numerous examples of the romantic ideal of the ghost. One folk song originating in the late 18th century, "Sweet William's Ghost," had a ghost begging his beloved to free him from his promise to her. Without her permission, he would be forever damned.

And speaking of England, let's take another step and see what kinds of ghosts we can find in the British isles. Lots and lots, as it turns out, but much of it with familiar origins in Europe. The ghosts we encounter in England are of Germanic origin with liberal dashes of Celtic flair. We're going to look at those Celts, first Ireland and then Scotland.

*Bean sidhe*
We've heard so much about the *bean sidhe* (pronounced "banshee" and meaning "woman of the sidhe") of Ireland. Who is she? She is a female spirit, a messenger from the land of the dead, and is the omen of death. The Scottish

Gaels know her as the *bean sith*, and there are similar ghost creatures in Welsh lore, Norse lore, and in American folklore. This creature isn't evil, simply a harbinger of a coming death, and despite her screaming that chills men's souls to alert the coming demise, for the most part she appears to deliver the dying to the afterlife, much in the same way that the soul bird delivers the dead in Finnish mythology and Hermes accompanies the Greek dead to the river Styx.

Numerous stories in Irish lore have differing bean sidhe origins, one of which says that the bean sidhe came to be when a young woman was murdered in such a horrible way that her ghost still wanders, warning members of her family that another violent death is coming. But this wanders off the traditional origins for the bean sidhe, because more common bean sidhe origin stories call for the ghost to simply warn for a death of a family member, not necessarily in a violent fashion.

There are variations of bean sidhe. One appears as an elderly woman dressed in rags and with long gray, silver, or white hair, long fingernails and sharp decaying teeth or face covered with a black veil, screaming to chill men's souls. When you can see her face, her eyes are said to be blood red and to look at them directly will cause insanity or death (so in this case, causing death instead of warning about it), not to mention her continuously open mouth, because her scream not only warns (and terrifies) the living, it tortures them too. Sometimes she is never seen, only heard, with her terrifying scream. Sometimes she appears as a young red-haired woman dressed in a shroud, always screaming. So keep an ear out for that cry. And run the other way!

Another kind of bean sidhe delights in torturing the

living and taking their souls, often stalking their intended victim with their screams, driving them insane and finally to death. This kind has even been known to tear her victim apart. Now this kind of banshee is what you want to avoid!

And then there are the shapeshifting ghosts, as described by William Butler Yeats. As they're known in Ireland, the *thevshi*, or *tash*, are suspended between life and death because of something unfulfilled during life, whether affection or anger or revenge or even jealousy. The Irish are apparently comfortable with the constant threat of haunting by ghosts (except for the bean sidhe, since no one's comfortable with them), however.

In addition, Yeats quotes a Lady Wilde about the dead being kept from their rest, or "waking the dog that watches to devour the souls of the dead," not unlike the Greeks' Cerberus, the three-headed dog that strips the newly dead down to their skeletons when they arrive in the underworld. For the Irish, however, those who die abruptly are more likely to become ghosts that haunt the living, acting as poltergeists.

Sometimes the local faeries waylay the soul from the dying body and spirit it away (sorry) from its rightful resting place. Unfortunately, these souls are unable to find their way back and are referred to as lost souls. Children are particularly in danger of this.

Those who die and who during life was considered to be too bad to ascend to heaven but too good for hell are doomed to remain on Earth as a ghost, according to another Irish legend. They are forced to obey the living, specifically someone they did wrong to, as a servant for an indefinite time. Contrast this with other ghost servants throughout the world (in Slavic culture, Japanese, and Asia Pacific, for example), but in those cases, the ghosts mostly serve as multigenerational family retainers.

And of course, Irish ghost lore holds that the dead are also known to shapeshift and appear as animals or insects, butterflies in particular, around areas where they lived. They may appear as a rat, a cat, a black dog, or even an elf. If you see butterflies, that's a good thing. Butterflies fluttering around a funeral rite are said to be a sign that the soul will rest in peace and not come back to haunt the living.

Irish ghosts that manifest as poltergeists (or, as the Irish just refer to them, the noisy ghosts) tend to make themselves known in a residence at night, and they can reside in a large tree that may grow next to the residence. While such ghosts don't tend to be all that bright, for the most part they are friendly, though mischievous. If the living residents make the mistake of angering the ghost, it could become vengeful, sickening the livestock, causing drought, or even attempting to cause harm to the humans. When this occurs, only when the residence itself has been destroyed will the ghost leave.

*Elsewhere In Europe…*
During the Victorian period, ghosts became popular in European culture, less something to be frightened of but more a curiosity. Spiritualism in the US (known as *spiritism* in Europe) developed in the mid-1800s and surged in popularity until the early 20th century, with almost 10 million adherents to the craze.

**Consider This:** Do you have family ghost stories that sound vaguely like those we've covered so far?

# Chapter 5
*Blurring Ghost Lines in Slavic Land*

As we travel south in Europe, we begin to encounter more and more instances of the dead coming back to threaten the living. There are those who would take the blood of the living (the *strigoi* and the vampire), and then there are those who seek revenge. Ghosts and vampires blur lines as we travel to the Slavic states, and of course Romania, which has a distinctive scary ghost tradition of its own.

In Slavic lore, a *rusalka* (plural *rusalki*) is a ghost of a young woman who died violently, often a suicide (either jilted or pregnant and unmarried) or murder, often by drowning in a river, a lake, or a pond. Rusalki are also known to take the form of a water spirit or a mermaid. Those bodies of water are often known to be haunted by the rusalki. This particular kind of ghost is not generally hostile, and will no longer act up if their unjust deaths are avenged. Rusalki are also thought to be those young women who died abrupt and violent deaths without proper funeral rites. As we take our journey around the world, you'll find that the proper death ceremonies of the culture will do wonders to calm down unquiet spirits, no matter where you are.

The unquiet dead of the rusalka isn't the only type of ghost known in Slavic culture. There's the *domovoi*, who works sort of like a ghost cop, devoted to keeping order for a household. In certain areas, every home has one to pitch in with chores or act as a limited guardian angel for the family.

This concept of a family ghost pops up around the world, so it must be an idea that appeals to many cultures; we'll find a reference to ghosts as family servants in Japan and elsewhere in Asia Pacific, the spirits handed down from generation to generation. The ghost servant in Slavic folklore is also a shapeshifter, usually showing up as a small hairy male human (this may remind you of an elf in Celtic cultures, where—no surprise!—they act as guardian angel and housekeeper) but also known to show up as a cat or a dog (also see the Celts).

Of course, if you get on the wrong side of the domovoi, look out. It can lash out like a poltergeist, throwing things around and (worse, for a ghost who pitches in with the chores) leaving muddy footprints!

Romanian folklore is more than the legend of the vampire. In fact, it seems to be filled with dark lore, including a Wikipedia entry on the most haunted forests of the region.

Among the legends inspiring the reputation is the one about the Trivale Forest, where the daughter of a wealthy landowner ran away with a servant. The father tracked them down, killed the servant...and then cut his daughter's head off. The headless ghost of the bride haunts the forest still.

Then for those who are gambling enthusiasts, consider

this: Vernescu House is the site of a casino where, in the past decades, players have committed suicide after they gambled their fortunes away. Three ghosts apparently haunt the house, shaking the furniture, shift the air currents, and even appear in the hallways. The smell of sulfur has also been reported on the premises.

Finally, we have a kind of ghost in Romanian folklore that may hint at how vampires became so indelibly connected to the region, when ghosts are persuaded to come back to join the living by pouring warm, newly extracted blood onto the ground. Once this was done, the ghost could rejoin the living, but only stay that way by continuing to pour more warm blood on the ground from time to time in a rite. In this region, *strigoi* are known to be troubled dead, dating back about 3,000 years. They manifest as evil ghosts who haunt their living family. So even when Romanians try to get away from vampires, these ghosts keep bringing them back!

**Consider This:** What do you think Scandinavian ghosts have in common with Romanian ones?

Image of Cerberus, the three-headed dog of Greek myth.

# Chapter 6
*Greek and Roman Ghosts*

With all the hubbub and excitement about the gods of the Greeks and the Romans, the ghosts of these cultures are often overlooked. Which is too bad, because there's a whole lot of ghost lore between these two, and in fact, a lot of what we think of as ghost lore comes from these two cultures.

First of all, ghosts of the Greek and the Roman varieties are referred to as *shades*. Because the Romans appropriated a great deal of their philosophy and religion from the Greeks, I'll mostly refer to the Greeks. But interestingly, the Romans had their own distinct ghost culture.

To start with, Hecate was a goddess in Greek mythology known for her association with many things, including the moon, fire, magic, ghosts, witchcraft, herbage, and plants. She oversaw the earth, sea, and sky, was known as the mother of angels and the "cosmic world soul," and she was also known as the protector of households and families. Of course, Hades was lord of the underworld, in charge of the souls of the dead (yes, the land was named after the lord). So Hecate was in charge specifically of the shades, but he was in charge of the dead. If the shades manifested on our plane of existence, she would have control, but if they stayed in the underworld, Hades was still in charge. Fine distinction there, but important to the Greeks. Not only that, to avenge those who died unjustly, the Erinyes, the goddesses of the dead, were known to inflict madness on the survivors and even cause starvation and plague.

Then there were the shades themselves. Homer described ghosts in his *Odyssey* and the *Iliad*, but unlike spirits found in other cultures, the earliest Greek ghosts weren't to be particularly feared, described as insubstantial at best (often appearing as smoke; this isn't the only culture to have ghosts manifest this way), on occasion offering advice, although they were known to be easily annoyed (yes, that's right, cranky ghosts).

It was only later that Greek ghosts became scary beings who could be good or evil, becoming a nuisance on occasion. These later ghosts were appeased with annual festivals to honor them, particularly those ghosts with families still in existence; the shades were invited back to Earth for that particular time. If their family line had been extinguished, though, their power was either extinguished or minimized sharply.

This idea appears elsewhere in the world when it comes to the power inherent in ghosts, that they have power only if their lineage remains. Otherwise, they are forgotten and powerless and gone, gone, gone. This idea of a "ghost festival" appears fairly often in various cultures around the world in varying places like Mexico, in their Day of the Dead celebration, the Chinese festival of the ghosts, and Japan, with their Bon Odori celebration, and of course, Halloween.

The Greek underworld was their idea of an afterlife, the final unresting place for their dead. After a human died and left the corporeal form of his or her body, he or she made their way to the rivers of the dead, taken there by Hermes. There were a few rivers of the dead; the rivers Styx and Acheron were those that the newly dead were ferried across by the boatman Charon to get to Hades and his dominion. You may vaguely remember the stories about the bodies of the dead being given a coin, to pay the ferryman for the journey. (The other rivers: Lethe, the river of forgetfulness; Phlegethon, the river of fire; and Cocytus, the river of sorrow.) (And recall that the Finns had their own ferryman to the underworld.)

Then, of course, there was the three-headed beast Cerberus, whose job was to strip away the human forms of the newly arrived dead and bring them down to skeletons, thus achieving equality, down to our very bones. (Remember the old saying how we're all equal when we're dead? Yes, this is pretty much how it is.)

The Greeks got pretty detailed about the lands of the dead, among which were Tantalus, even below the underworld, where the Titans dwelled; the Fields of Asphodel, where those who didn't make much of an impression one way or another during life ended up; and of course, if the newly dead did make an impression—a good one—during life, they ended up in the Elysian Fields. (Those who ended up in Asphodel could work their way up, and even if you ended up in Elysian, if you *really* worked, you could work your way up to the Isles of the Blessed, the super-duper level.)

The Greek play *Oresteia*, written circa fifth-century BC, had one of the first ghosts included as a character, so

Shakespeare's Banquo came from a long tradition.

From the Greeks we have the familiar tale of Orpheus and Eurydice, an early example we have of a grieving lover following a beloved even into the land of the dead. If you recall the story, Orpheus lost his bride Eurydice on their wedding day when a poisonous snake bit her, but he managed to persuade Hades and his wife Persephone to let him retrieve her. But they had one condition: when he did get her, he could not look back at the underworld as they ascended to the land of the living.

You know the rest of the story. He did, and she had to go back to the land of the dead.

This story isn't unique; there is at least one with similar themes in Native American lore, and one in some African cultures, perhaps from the same source, although the African story is at its heart the story of someone who's wandered into the wrong place. We'll look at that story soon.

Then there are the Romans. So many details they lifted from the Greeks, yet they had unique ghost lore on their own. The way we think of many ghost stories has their origins in how the ancient Romans viewed them, with the haunting of physical places with those murdered. The philosopher Pliny the Younger recounted the story of a ghost bound by chains to a certain house and disturbing the living, to stop only when the skeleton was given a proper burial. The theme of proper rites and ceremonies for the dead show up in every single culture with stories about the dead. What's the moral of the story? Bury the dead properly! If you don't, you shouldn't be surprised if they rise, make you sick, try to eat you, or even just annoy the heck out of you. Burial rites are important!

The Roman ghosts were split into distinct types. Some of them were generally friends to the living, while some tended to be easily aggravated (like those cranky Greek ghosts). Like any culture with ghost lore, the Romans had ceremonies and rites for keeping the dead at bay.

There was a holiday called Lemuria, according to the philosopher Ovid, taken from a festival called Remuria begun by Romulus to appease the ghost of his brother Remus. Roman ghosts were described as generally shapeless, as opposed to the Greek shades, who for the most part were described as skeletons, having had their human forms stripped away when they arrived in the underworld (taken by the three-headed beast Cerberus).

**Consider This:** Do you think that the jima of the Amazon and the Greek underworld dog Cerberus are related in any way?

Kolelo, a serpent ancestral ghost believed to have a role in
the Maji Maji Rebellion.

# Chapter 7
*Ghosts in Darkest Africa*

An entire continent of ghosts, barely dead. That's what ghosts in Africa are viewed as, according to much of the literature on the subject, and that makes sense, considering it's an ancient continent with multiple, layered cultures and multiple, layered histories.

Ghosts are everywhere in Africa, from the top of the continent all the way to the bottom. Somewhere in the middle is the Bantu culture, the core of which is the cult of the dead, where the dead are honored and treated as something virtually godlike, with abilities beyond those of mortal men. Then there are the *adze*, the vampire-like ghosts of the people of Ewe in Ghana, who hold an obsessive fascination about humans and suck the blood of small children.

In the beliefs of many African cultures, souls continue to exist beyond the death of the body and they continue to have a say in the manner in which the living conduct their daily affairs. To communicate the opinions of the dead, there are signs unique to each society and those who specialize in communicating with the ancestors. Make sure you're polite in your references to the dead, because there could be repercussions if the ghosts are offended somehow.

This too seems to be universal in cultures anywhere along the Silk Road and beyond: if you believe in ghosts, you have to maintain a peace with them.

In African cultures, however, the soul or ghost is not generally believed to exist indefinitely. In a familiar twist of a phrase, the spirits exist only as long as they are remembered by the living and in addition, existence may continue only as long as the culture or the familial line exists.

But that isn't necessarily the philosophy that you can find everywhere. The Wazaramo of Tanganyika have *makungu*, the ghosts of the male members of a family. After a certain period of time they merge into a category of spirits referred to as *vinyamkela* (thought to be children or inoffensive male adults) or *majini* (thought to be violent males). (And no, we didn't find anything about the females. But we'll keep looking.)

*Majini* is a borrowed term from the Arabic-origin *djinn*, and is relatively modern; an earlier term is *dzedzeta*, or *mwene mbago* (meaning "lord or lady of the forest"). The mwene mbago is invisible and lives in hollow trees. There are exorcists referred to as "doctors" to get rid of the mwene mbago. (Yes, as in "witch doctors.")

Also invisible is the *kimyamkela* (the singular form for vimyamkela), but when it chooses to appear, it only does so as half a human, with one leg, one hand, one eye, and one ear. This half business also appears elsewhere in world mythology. These ghosts hang out near their graves and what were their homes before they make the final crossover to the afterlife. Like many other ghost cultures, the

Wazaramo believe their departed live the way they did for the most part as they did when they were alive. Like some other ghost cultures, the Wazaramo consider their departed spirits to be tricksters. Those ghost jokesters!

Another belief common in this region, as well as others, is the idea of the recently deceased to reveal themselves in the form of various animals. The Atonga believe that taking certain herbal concoctions allow them to shapeshift into whatever they choose after death, with their tribal leaders coming back as lions and their tribal shamans into something like leopards and hyenas. Also found in this area are stories about the dead coming back as birds; you'll find this theme pretty common in the Pacific Rim as well, and even in places as far away as Finland (think of the soul bird).

The "ghost country"—where, according to many African cultural beliefs, the ghosts hang out after death—is generally thought to be underground, often reached through caves and holes in the ground, with the dead leading for the most part similar lives as they did alive.

The Wakuluwe hold that their ghosts live in a village at the center of the Earth; this place is referred to as *mosima*, or the abyss. According to the Bapedi, the entry to the ghost country could be found on their lands and entered using a simple ritual. (You have to find the entryway first, of course.) The ghost country can also be reached on Mt. Kilimanjaro by diving into certain pools of water or certain caves. In a story with a common theme as others we'll find around the world, including some vaguely similar elements in common with the Greek tale of Orpheus, there is a tale about a man who is thought to be dead who makes his way to the ghost country, but when the ghosts he meets there ignore him and indicate they believe he does not belong there, he comes back.

And speaking of trips to the land of the dead, in a story from the Wachaga comes how a girl reached the land of the ghosts and returned to the land of the living. A girl named Marwe slipped into a pool and inadvertently found the entry to the country of the ghosts at the bottom. Before she went very far in her exploration, she came upon an old woman who lived in a hut with many children, and the woman invited her to stay with them. They offered her food but always Marwe refused, knowing that those who reach the land of the ghosts who partake of the food must stay there. (Does this sound familiar? There are variations of this all over the world.) One day she decides it was time for her to go home, and tells the old woman so, but then the woman asks her if she wants to be hit with the cold or the hot?

Marwe, understandably, is mystified, but chooses the cold. The woman tells her to dip her arms into a pot, and when she brings them back up, finding them covered with bangles. She is told to do the same with her feet, and brings them back up with her ankles covered with jewelry wrought of ornate brass and copper chains. The old woman tells her that her future husband is named Sawoye, and he will take her home. And so Marwe goes back up to the surface. The villagers find her by the pool, covered with ornate jewelry. The chief of the village offers to take her home, but she refuses, as she is waiting for the man the old woman said would be taking her.

Eventually, Sawoye appears and identifies himself, and Marwe allows herself to be taken home by this man and married to him. Apparently her parents, even though this is all very odd, had no objections. But then, it's not very often that someone comes back from the land of the dead, covered with ornate jewelry and having had her future husband chosen by the chieftain of the ghosts.

Finally, the Wazaramo have a serpent god called Kolelo, believed to be an ancestral ghost. He was featured in the troubled history of the area, in the 1905 Maji Maji Rebellion in German East Africa. So local ghosts and ancestors can also play a part in wars.

**Consider This:** If you believed that the ghost of your ancestor turned into an animal, which ancestor would you say it was and what would the animal be?

The soul was represented in ancient Egyptian culture by the khu, represented as a crested ibis, most likely a homonym.

# Chapter 8
*Through the Middle and Near East,*
*We See Ghosts*

While Egypt is part of the African continent (it is; go take a look), we're looking at its ghost culture as more connected with the Middle East and Near East because its history and culture have more in common with those. And we do have to look at Egyptian culture. Come on, it's the Egyptian Book of the Dead, we *need* to look at it! Anyway.

Ghosts are a big part of the ancient Egyptian culture, with their belief in the afterlife the source of so much fiction. Those ideas about the dead and their existence were compiled into (of course) the Egyptian Book of the Dead, in the form of papyrus scrolls and pyramid paintings. It should be noted that these beliefs come from different periods of Egyptian history over a span of almost 3,000 years. The title, of course, is a misnomer; it's not a single book, it's a series of them, all with different themes, but all with the central idea that there is an existence after death.

The concept of the soul was represented in ancient Egyptian culture by the *khu*, represented as a crested ibis. In the Greco-Roman periods, the khu was viewed as a demonic ghost, possessing the living.

Later on, the Egyptian culture broke down the concept of the soul into five parts: the soul/heart (the center of thought and/or emotion), the shadow (a person couldn't live without one), the name (something as necessary to survive as a shadow or soul, it would be bestowed at birth and would protect against harm), the *ba* (basically, personality), and the spirit, or life itself (*ka*). When the ka leaves, the person officially dies. The personality (ba) and life (ka) combine after death to form the *akh*—essentially, a ghost. Provided the correct rites are performed, the ba and ka could be brought back to life at a later time. The akh could wreak havoc or calm a hazardous situation to the living, depending on the circumstances. One way or another, the life of the person continued.

The idea of eternal life, of course, is not unique to the Egyptians; the interpretation of the concept is what differs from region to region. In this case, the spirit was believed to live in the tomb where the body was, so servants were killed to accompany the wealthy and noble decedents to make the afterlife as similar to their lives; food too was included in the tomb, because they'd be hungry when they came back to life. How's that, you say? They're dead! That's where the Book of the Dead comes in.

Now, the Egyptians truly understood the importance of funeral rituals. When the wealthy and the nobility died, there were hymns and directions provided in their tombs designed to aid them in the next plane of existence, which is, as you might have figured out, how the Book of the Dead came about, with specific texts specifically for the pharaoh. Those texts—meant to be magical spells—provided all kinds of ways for the ruler to come back to life in one way or another, meet the gods, how he could travel, and so forth. (Interesting ghostly tidbit: Akhenaten, the pharaoh who ruled from approximately 1353 BCE to 1335 BCE, was cursed by the local priests who were offended by his attempt to establish his own religion. After his death, he was doomed to wander as a ghost through the desert for eternity, and apparently there are those who claim to have encountered him from time to time.)

But the ancient Egyptian civilization wasn't the only ancient culture in the Middle and Near East with ghosts. The Mesopotamian cultures (such as Sumer, Babylon, and Assyria, to name only a few) had their own.

Back in the Mesopotamian Age…so to speak…ghosts were as big as they are now. Whether Sumerian, Babylonian, Assyrian, or others, ghosts played an important part of the culture. Ghosts were known as *gidim* in Sumerian, and as *etemmu* in Akkadian. Gidim maintained the personality of the deceased and upon arriving in the underworld, resumed a day-to-day existence much like theirs during their lives. But before they could get to the underworld in Babylonian myth, known as Irkalla, the deceased had to overcome a series of hurdles.

Like the spirits of other cultures, both near and far, ghosts in this region are virtual copies of the lifer, with personality and memory intact; they're just not alive. (In some cultures, however, ghosts may not remember their previous lives.) They received offerings of food and drink, and if they were displeased with what they got, they took revenge, with terrible illness inflicted on the living often ascribed to the dead (on the other hand, if they were happy, they bestowed good things). Even the Bible has some references to ghosts; in the Old Testament, one is in the first book of Samuel, where the Witch of Endor summons the ghost of Samuel. And in the Talmud, there is a reference to a shade that lives and dies but cannot be seen.

Then there's the New Testament, in which Jesus is mistaken for a ghost when he comes back after the resurrection. Abrahamic beliefs generally hold that ghosts are those who have passed on but are for some reason tied to this plane of existence; some religious denominations view ghosts as those who are in a purgatory, waiting before going to their next stage of existence, while others believe ghosts are demons and thus impure.

And speaking of the Abrahamic tradition, its afterlife belief has a lot in common with that of many other traditions. The story of crossing the river Jordan to reach the promised land echoes the use of water—specifically, a river—for the newly deceased to reach either the land of the afterlife is a variation of those that we encounter all around the world. Water is important for cultures, no matter the form.

How far back does that go? There's the old, old story of Gilgamesh, perhaps the oldest known, between 5,000 to 10,000 years old. In it, ol' Gil is searching for the secret behind immortality and he runs into a ferryman (yes, again!) whom he persuades or tricks into taking him across the waters of death. Considering how old this particular story is makes me wonder if it's the original about this topic.

Then there is Islam, which doesn't officially recognize ghosts. What they recognize instead are the *djinn*. (Djinn are the all-around folklore figure in these parts; they can be ghosts, demons, faeries.) Like ghosts, they are known to come about after death and gain certain abilities at that point. There are various forms of djinn, some of whom are malevolent, some of whom are not. In Persian folklore (that is, before the introduction of Islam), there was the *bakhtak*, a malevolent ghost that can cause sleep paralysis.

**Consider This:** Can you imagine Robin Williams playing a ghost instead of a djinn?

Demonic ghost from Hindu myth.

# Chapter 9
*In India and the Subcontinent of Ghosts*

Next, our travels take us to the Indian subcontinent (or the Pako-Indio-Bangladesh subcontinent, to be politically accurate) and the region thereof, which roughly takes into account yes, Pakistan, India, and Bangladesh—in short, what was once British India. The description also takes into account Nepal, Bhutan, Sri Lanka, Tibet, and sometimes even Afghanistan. But no matter what nations and cultures are or aren't included in this overview, one thing is certain: there are ghost myths.

To start with, there's the *bhut*, a restless ghost, according to Hindu culture and throughout the area. These are the spirits that are somehow prevented from passing onto the next step of existence, whether because of a violent death, previous life with turmoil, or the lack of proper death rituals (remember, no matter where you go, a lot of threatening creatures, ghosts, vampires, or more, seem to come about because of improper or lack of funeral rites). There are many other alarming spirits in Hindu mythology; among others, there is the *baital*, an evil being who specifically haunts cemeteries and takes possession of corpses that went without proper funerary rites. Again, those rites are important to keep the dead in peaceful slumber.

In Hindu culture, ghosts are generally referred to as *preta*. As in ancient Egyptian culture, in Hindu tradition there is the concept of the soul split apart from the physical body, referred to as *kshooshma shareera*. In *kshooshma shareera,* the five senses of the living being are imprinted on the soul, and this impression is carried away by the soul when death occurs. The proper funeral rites ensure that the lingering soul impressions are expunged from the living world, thus releasing the soul to the next existence.

Spirit guides have their part to play in central and northern India in the form of the *ojha* (a more familiar term is "exorcist"). The term is derived from the archaic language of Sanskrit and roughly translates as "those who control the spirits on Earth." The term and spirit guide theme can also be found in Nepalese culture.

The less famous book of the dead, *Bardo Thodol*, also known as the Tibetan Book of the Dead, is a funerary text, like the Egyptian Book of the Dead (and like the Egyptian Book of the Dead, isn't a book per se, but a series of works on the same theme). Unlike the Egyptian version, the Tibetan version guides the dying and dead through the entire process of death before rebirth. (This period is referred to as the *bardo*. *Thodol* means "liberation," and the formal name of the work literally translates as "Social Liberation of the Hearing.") The Bardo Thodol also details the signs of death (multiple chapters' worth), and the rituals to perform when death is imminent or has occurred (as we have noted, bad things happen if you don't do the rituals).

With a well-established document of death and death rites and preparing for the next life, it's clear that Tibetan culture also has a well-established belief in ghosts. While Buddhism per se doesn't recognize the existence of ghosts in its philosophy, Tibetan Buddhism does (there are many different types of Buddhism, as you may have gathered) and is the source of many local ghost legends.

The legend of the hungry ghost (which you may or may not be familiar with, but it is famous in Chinese culture and also throughout Asia) can also be found in Tibetan culture. In Tibetan culture, ghosts with a malevolent nature can be trapped or exorcised with a sanctified dagger, allowing them to continue onto their next plane of existence. An annual festival has been held in Tibet in the past for this purpose. There is the tale of a ghost of a 17th-century monk named Dorje Shugden who is regarded as a deity by some, but the Dalai Lama disagrees, calling him an evil spirit.

In other Buddhist-based cultures like Bhutan, officially, there is no belief in ghosts—but local folklore always has a story or two. Wherever you go…

Then in Hindu mythology, there's the river Vaitaran, which marks the boundary between the living and the dead. In Hindu tradition, there are places along the river that makes it easier for the newly deceased to cross. There's that thing about rivers and the deceased again!

Sometimes the ghost myths in a culture can be minor. Despite the general Muslim rejection of ghosts—because, as you may recall, Islamic teachings say there are no such thing as ghosts—they can be considered to be djinn; in addition, backward feet on a corpse or a suspicious-looking person could indicate a witch or a ghost in disguise.

**Consider This:** How important are funeral rites?

Japanese woodblock print of a female ghost.

# Chapter 10
*The East Asian Triangle: The Ghosts of China, Korea, and Japan*

Ghost myths are all over, and that includes China. And Korea. And all of Asia, come to think of it. The Chinese myth of the hungry ghost is well known, all around the globe; in fact, it was the underlying plot for an episode of *The X-Files*. In the story of the hungry ghost, the ghost is continually starving because it has been cursed with a huge empty stomach but a tiny mouth, so it can never consume enough. The festival of the hungry ghost involves various methods of attempting to mollify the ghost, with money or food.

There are many different kinds of ghosts in Asian culture, depending on where you are, how the decedent met his or her fate, and quite often whether these spirits mean harm to the living (they don't, not all of them, and not all the time). And because Chinese cultural beliefs are everywhere in Asia, there's quite a bit of overlap. So it's not uncommon to find the same folktales all over Asia, with names sometimes changed and sometimes not. Finding the variations can be a fun challenge.

First of all, the Chinese have a tradition of ancestor worship (in Taoism, Confucianism, and the local version of

Buddhism, but not Communism, of course) associated with ghost beliefs. After all, who else is going to haunt you, really, but someone close to you? (Well, there may be others, but in Chinese culture ancestor ghosts are most common.) Ghosts are referenced frequently in Chinese scholarly works, both classic and modern. And it's not just in academic treatises, either; recent surveys indicate that about 90% of the Chinese still believe in ghosts, even in Communist China.

There are numerous ghost myths in Chinese culture, and a glance at the list will give you a clue that Chinese culture and its ghosts have spread far and wide in various forms. Some examples of Chinese ghosts are drought ghosts, who were consumed by lust in life and now are responsible for hot winds that can destroy the crops; trickster ghosts who are, well, tricksters, and can transform into animals in order to play pranks; venomous ghosts, who were hateful during their lives and after dying transform into insects and continue to annoy the living. In addition, there are Chinese ghosts that cause disease and decay like the Scandinavian *draugrs* because their bitter nature in life carried over into their afterlife.

Some Chinese spirits are less malevolent, like the servant ghost (like the Japanese *shikigami* and the *domovoi* of Slavic folklore, ghosts that act as servants to families, passed down through generations, also found in Pacific Rim ghost myths), but the Chinese servant ghost is unique in its ability to transform into light. (Yes, a servant who's light itself! Okay, yeah, that's odd.)

Then there's the story of the ghost who is good company, in the story of the drinking companions. A man who regularly attempts to fish in a river near his village to support his family, but he's not very good at it. Then one day he notices a nervous-looking man nearby, who seems to have no purpose there. The would-be fisherman always pours a little wine into the swift waters to share with the victims of the strong current, and so, he offers some to the nervous man to share with him. After that, they become friendly companions, sharing wine alongside the river as the terrible fisherman and the nervous man get chummy. The nervous-looking man turns out to be a ghost, of course, and as a reward for his friendliness the fisherman prospers after the ghost eventually is reborn.

And remember the hungry ghost, mentioned earlier? According to the *Dictionary of Chinese Buddhist Terms*, there are various types of hungry ghosts, which include torch-mouth ghosts, which have mouths like burning torches in punishment for their poor behavior in life; needle-mouth ghosts, the traditional hungry ghost you may have heard about, with tiny mouths so their hunger can never be satisfied; foul-mouth ghosts, who have terrible, horrible breath; which is in the same category as the smelly-haired ghost, who has…well, you get the idea. Also of note are the ghosts that consume life energy and eat leftovers, and the ghosts of powerful rulers, who were violent in life and remain that way in the afterlife.

And there's the traditional ghost festival, observed by Chinese all over the world and in various forms. (In Japan, there's the Bon Odori, which is celebrated at approximately the same time of the year. More on that later.) In the Chinese ghost festival, the ancestors come back to this plane of existence to greet their descendants and in general have a party. There's an account of this festival by a Japanese visitor in 840, so it's been celebrated for at least a thousand years or so.

There's another tale about the living visiting the dead, like the Greek, the Bapedi, the Wachaga, and the Native American Piegan, but this time from the Chinese. In the legend of Moginlin, a man wants to save his mother from starvation in the underworld. (A happy afterlife? Not necessarily.) He journeys to the underworld to provide her with food—but the food is forever unobtainable for her. He doesn't know what he can do for her, but he prays to the Buddha, and finally, the Buddha tells Moginlin to find monks who will fast and pray with him in the middle of the seventh month. He does so, and in this way, Moginlin frees his mother from her afterlife starvation. (The Japanese version of this story is about Moku-ren, who also endeavors to help his late mother.)

Now we step over to Korean mythology, which consists of not only lore with Chinese origins, but those with origins from other points. Like other countries (in)conveniently situated between warring cultures, Korea tended to get invaded a lot in the long ago, which means that the resulting culture is rich with legends from a number of cultures, shaped into a distinctive whole. One of the main ancestor beliefs in Korean culture, like Japanese culture, is a form of animism, which is essentially the worship of nature. So there are spirits everywhere in Korean culture like Japanese culture, both ancestors and nature haunting the living.

In Korean culture, ghosts are generally known as *gwishin*, the souls of the departed. According to Wikipedia, some specific Korean ghosts are categorized as *mool-gwishin*, the ghost of a drowning victim, a water ghost with stretchy arms to entrap its victims; *cheo-nyeo-gwishin*, the ghost of a virgin (or unmarried) woman; *mong-dal-gwishin* or *ching gak gwishin*, an unmarried man (indicating that marriage is a preferable state in Korea); the *jeoseung saja*, the grim reaper ghost, and finally, *dal-gyal-gwishin*, a ghost from an unspecified death who has no eyes, nose, or mouth, the faceless ghost.

Like similar ghosts of other cultures, *gwishin* are those who for one reason or another are unable to pass to the next plane of existence. Many rituals in Korean culture have been devised to address an unquiet death, to ease the disturbed spirit to the other side. (What did we say? Funeral rituals are important!)

The *cheo-nyeo-gwishin*, the ghost of an unmarried woman, is notable for the traditional white robe in which she appears, the classic Korean woman's shroud. In Korean society, an unmarried woman is considered to be of low status, and a ghost of one wears her hair down (wearing her hair up is considered a privilege). The male equivalent is referred to as a "bachelor ghost."

Because a state of unweddedness can be enough to keep ghosts restless, on rare occasions "soul weddings" are held for the unmarried departed so the spirits may be at peace. In the ABC TV show *Dr. Ken*, the 2016 Halloween episode, "D.R.'s Korean Ghost Story," did a good job of introducing some of these Korean ghosts to the American audience, so if you ever get a chance, check it out (probably available on YouTube, at least for some of the pertinent ghosts).

And of course, Korean ghosts, like others in Asia, can also be depicted as floating, legless, and see-through.

Then there's Japan. Japanese culture is famous for its fascination with ghosts and has many ghost stories, some of which were immortalized in the various works of a 19th-century Irish/Greek-American storyteller named Lafcadio Hearn, whose books are still available today. Hearn was a wandering journalist, and if you're ever in New Orleans, there is a historic note outside of a building where he lived for a while as he worked as a reporter for a local newspaper. He gained fame for essentially shaping how we see New Orleans today with his articles, books, and even a cookbook. But he was restless, and after a decade or so, he moved on.

Eventually Lafcadio Hearn ended up in Japan, where he became a Japanese citizen, married a Japanese woman, and taught at Tokyo Imperial University (now known as University of Tokyo), famous for his Western exploration into Japanese myth. One of the books he wrote for a Western audience about Japanese society was a collection of ghost stories, *Kwaidan*, which was adapted into a movie in the early 1960s.

In *The Book of Yokai* by Michael Dylan Foster, he posits that ghosts in Japanese culture are basically two kinds. First are people who have died harboring an attachment to something or someone or has unfinished business. They wander around among the living like they did in life. If you didn't realize they were dead, you would assume they were just odd. They may have become this sort of *yokai* (a term for ghost or monster) because of a sudden death, and so they are unable to make peace with the world.

Then there is the second type of Japanese ghost, according to Foster, which appears as someone who had clearly passed on and is dressed in a shroud and may appear without feet, indicating they are not grounded in the earthly plain. Both kinds are associated with a specific person who lived, not a vague presence. (Both echo what we've found in

Chinese and Korean mythologies.)

The Japanese have a long tradition of monsters and ghosts. There are so many different kinds of Japanese ghosts. Here are examples of only a few:

In Japanese folklore, *yurei* is a form of ghost. This term means "faint spirit." (Another common term is *obake*, which also means ghost or monster, sometimes used as a variation of boogeyman.) Other terms are *borei*, "ruined spirit," and *shiryo*, "dead spirit." Like their Chinese counterparts (and ghosts all around the world), Japanese ghosts are thought to be souls kept from a peaceful nether existence (again, possibly because of unfinished business, improper funerary rites, or a violent death).

But wait, there's more! Possession is a common theme. There's the *bakechochin*, which is a ghost that manifests as a lantern with spirits trapped within. They are ghosts with a definite agenda, demon spirits, with long tongues and scary crazy eyes, ghosts of those who died with hate in their hearts. Because of this enduring hate, they are cursed to wander for all eternity. Stay away from these lanterns, because if you try to light one, one of these evil spirits may attack you!

Perhaps connected with the *bakechochin* is the *ikiryoh*, a ghost that results from the evil thoughts of a person who dies, again with hate in his or her heart. The *ikiryoh* can be so powerful that it can possess the living person who is the target of that hatred and slowly kill the person by draining his or her life energy (see Jacquie and Eilis's upcoming book on vampires, since a psychic vampire is one of four types we found). This kind of ghost is apparently very hard to get rid of, and of course there are many rites to do so, including numerous Buddhist sutras (scriptures).

And speaking of ghosts that hide in objects, there's the *mononoke*, which can be found in temples, shrines, and cemeteries, and it delights in scaring people to death. Again, sutras are written to get rid of them.

Then there's the *buruburu*. The name itself is onomatopoeiaic, for the sound of someone shivering; this type of ghost haunts forests and cemeteries disguised as an elderly person, sometimes appearing to have only one eye. It can cause an uncontrollable chill in a passerby, or even scare the person to death.

Ghosts whose heads are detached from their bodies show up a lot in Japanese horror stories (if you're an enthusiast of such things), and they are sometimes referred to as demons as well as ghosts. There's the headless *kubikajiri*, which is referred to as a "head-eating ghost," who smells like blood and spends its time in cemeteries looking for its head. If it doesn't succeed, it tries to eat the heads of any living thing that passes by.

And what about the *konakijii*? It's the spirit of an infant who has been left to die in the woods (often because the family itself is starving, the child was forbidden for some circumstance, or the child could be cursed by its birth). In revenge, the *konakijii* tricks unsuspecting people to enter the forest with the sound of a crying baby, but the trick is revealed when the innocent picks up the baby and discovers the infant looks like an old man. The victim is crushed by the sudden weight of the baby. (Not unlike the *draugrs* in Scandinavia, if you'll recall, who rise from their graves and kill humans who would disturb their sleep and trespass the graveyard by crushing them.)

Then there's the *shojo*, which is a Japanese spirit known to haunt the sea. Like a landlocked goblin demon common in Japanese folklore found around temples, the *shojo* has bright red hair, but this one has nothing against humans. Like the goblin demon, the *shojo* spends a lot of time drinking (and dancing), so it's a convivial ghost, like the Viking counterpart.

Then there's the *shokujinki*, previously known as *jiki-ninki*, from Japanese Buddhism. These ghosts are the spirits of greedy people who are cursed to hunt down and eat human corpses.

What may be the most famous story in Hearn's *Kwaidan* is the tale about the *noppera-bo*, the faceless woman. In this one, a man was traveling along the road to Edo when he came across a crying woman. He tried to help her, but when she faced him, he realized she had no face. Alarmed, he ran away and kept running until he came to a soba vendor. As the terrified man told him about the incident, the vendor's face disappeared, revealing that he too was a *noppera-bo*.

There are variations of this tale in Japanese myths, but what is notable is that they are not limited to the long-ago Japan; *noppera-bo* sightings have been reported wherever the Japanese have settled, including the United States, most notably in Japan.

And finally, there's the *tsukumogami*, a ghost that everyone would welcome. The name translates roughly to "old tool spirit," and these ghosts clean house and fix things, just like a Western-style brownie, in the middle of the night. But take care of those tools, because if you don't, these spirits will take revenge on the sleeping humans.

Again, not unlike the *domovoi* in Slavic folklore and other servant ghosts around the world, keeping order for a household and pitching in with family chores. (Why can't we all find ghosts like these, we ask?)

Finally, some random notes: all over Asia are myths about feetless ghosts, the state of which indicates that they are no longer connected to the earth, and so they wander if they did not receive the proper rites (again those proper rituals. Don't forget those rituals, guys!). The Japanese have an annual celebration welcoming their dead back to Earth in the form of their Bon Odori (meaning "dance of the dead") celebration, like the Chinese ghost festival. In Japan, families of the dead invite them to come back and dance with them, and generally have a spiritual barbecue, but with real food. If you get a chance, check out one of these celebrations; many areas with notable Japanese populations will have them in the middle of the summer. The food is good and so is the dancing. (It's Japanese line dancing, and you just follow the leader. Honor your ancestors, people, and dance with them!)

And yes, there's a Japanese myth concerning a river to cross for the deceased.

According to local lore, in the northern part of Japan, there's a mountain (the name differs depending on where you hear this story) where the entrance to hell may be found. There's a stream said to be the Sanzu River, where the newly dead make their way to the afterlife. Known as the river of three crossings, this body of water marks the place between life and death, and relative difficulty in getting across it depends on how the person behaved during life (there may be a bridge, if you've been good, a ford, if you've been okay, but there might be snakes in those waters otherwise!). Legend says the entry into the underworld itself is said to be guarded by Jizo, the guardian god of children.

And remember the stories we mentioned about the Wachaga, in which a girl finds herself in the home of the chieftain ghost, and the Bapedi, in which a man finds his way to the afterlife (for the Bapedi, the "ghost country") by finding the right entrance at a particular point at a mountain? There is another version in Japan, but in the form of part of the cultural creation story.

In this legend, the god Izanagi goes to the afterlife after finding the entry in a famed mountain to search for his wife Izanami, who died during childbirth, but because she consumed food of the afterlife, she cannot return. There are other elements of the story (revenge, he can't look at her or look back toward the afterland in an attempt to leave with her) that can also be found in other myths such as the Greek story about Persephone. Every time we see a variation of this tale, the moral of the story is always "Don't look back." And yet we do, every time.

Finally, in the words of Confucius (whose philosophy spread all over East Asia): "Respect ghosts and gods, but keep away from them."

**Consider This:** Think of those ghosts in the US kids' cartoon series *Casper The Friendly Ghost*. Why do you think Casper had feet but his adversaries didn't? Did the creators know what that signified? Are we overthinking this?

# Chapter 11
*Ghosts, in the Deepest Jungles of the Pacific Rim*

Again, once we arrive in this part of the world, we see an exotic combination of many, many different cultures and religions all meeting here for a dazzling display—and some terrifying ghosts.

The animism that is the basis of many Asian cultures have given way to ghost lore by the time we get here. Here, we see glimpses of Hindu, Buddhist, and even Muslim faiths, although ghosts are not part of the latter two religions (again, officially). Stories about vampire ghosts known as *pontianak* and *penanggalan* can be found throughout the region, as well as the *manananggal* and *tiyanak*. (Jacquie and Eilis also mention these in their book of vampires.)

Not only are Hindu, Buddhist, and Muslim faiths represented in the Pacific Rim, we have in the mix Polynesian culture, of course. Ghosts are big in Polynesian cultures, and like the ghost cultures of other cultures, there is an afterlife (sometimes referred to here as the "skyworld") where the deceased go, or they could be stuck in the here and now. Like the Viking *spöke* and the Muslim djinn, ghosts here can wreak revenge on the living for a slight in the form of an illness, which must be eradicated through the efforts of the local religious leaders.

In Thailand, ghosts are also part of the local folklore, and their spirit stories are most likely quite old in their origin, since local anthropologists (hooray for anthropologists!) have determined that the ghost myths found there are based on oral tradition. There is one particular ghost especially feared in Thai culture, Phi Tai Hong, who died a gruesome death without funerary ritual, forcing him to haunt the jungles and villages during certain times of the year. And like the *bakhtak* of Persian folklore, there is the *phi am*, who is known to cause sleep paralysis.

Malaysian culture, like others in the Pacific Rim region (a lot of others—Wikipedia cites Indonesia, Brunei, Java, Sumatra, and Singapore, and more), has ghost lore that may have been driven at least in part by local animist beliefs (influenced by Hindu and Buddhist beliefs as well as Muslim ones). The term for ghost in this region is *hantu* (yes, so similar to the American Southern term "haint" and of course "haunt"), and yes, there are many ghost types, again thanks to the cultural variations. And once again, because of the Muslim influence, ghosts are sometimes categorized here as evil djinn.

Malay folklore holds that the soul, considered to be no larger than thumb-sized, can flit from place to place, much like an insect or a bird. It has the ability to leave the body for short periods of time before eventually leaving for good at the time of death, at which point it can linger. The soul can once again wreak vengeance if slighted, often in the form of sudden or unexplained illnesses, which could be cured by the local shaman by incantations or animal sacrifice, or even a dance. Malay tradition holds that the spirit of the deceased sticks around the grave for a full week before taking its leave.

Malay ghosts are also known for possessing the living and usually do their thing during the night, particularly during a full moon. Reminiscent of one's name being so important in the ancient Egyptian concept of the soul, one way to avoid being affected by such ghosts in Malay culture is for the people to change their names so that the ghost can't find them. And here's something else that's unique: Malay ghosts can be tempted by food. When the ghost shapeshifts into a solid creature in order to eat, at that point it can be destroyed. (At least it's unique in this region. In the Americas, there is a voudun tradition of enticing a demon into something like a live chicken so it can be killed at that point.)

And then there is a ghost tradition in this region that is related to previously high rates of stillbirths and pregnancy-related deaths. There are other mythical creatures stemming from both in this region. The *bajang* is a spirit that assures that the proper funeral rites are used over the grave of a stillborn infant because otherwise it will cause convulsions and fainting among those left alive. It is also known to attack living infants and small children. In earlier times, small children would be given fabric bracelets (usually black silk) to protect them against the bajang. Then there's the *pelesit*, a ghost created from the tongue of a freshly buried firstborn stillborn, the mother of whom is also the firstborn of her family. The pelesit is similar to the bajang, but the owner of the bajang—because in this culture, you can claim control of your ghost—is always a man, whereas the pelesit is always controlled by a woman.

There is a lot of crossover with ghosts and demons in this region, and that is certainly clear in the case of the *langsuir*, referred to as a ghost of a woman who died during childbirth, but is also known as a vampire indigenous to the region, or a demon (it is an all-around useful term for the local folklore). An alternate form of ghost is the *pontianak*, which results when a woman dies in childbirth and the child is stillborn. *Matianak*, *kuntilanak*, and *tiyanak* are other names for these creatures. And speaking of pregnant women, a Filipino ghost called a *manananggal* preys on them, using their poisonous, elongated tongue. This ghost was the villain on an episode of the TV show *Grimm*.

And here's another regional ghost related to pregnant women. The *toyol*, which is often translated as "goblin," is the ghost of a human fetus. These ghosts are usually described as naked or close to naked, with green or grayish skin, fangs, and pointed ears. And horribly mischievous. These spirits are usually in service to a powerful demon or a human and are known to be thieves, but they think like children, easily distracted by candy or toys. The demon or human to whom the toyol are in servitude may become wealthy, but at the expense of those close to him.

In this region, like others, shamans are often quite powerful; they can exorcise demon ghosts from the living afflicted and enslave those ghosts to boot. The power of the shamans over the spirits are similar to that of the Japanese *shikigami*, ghosts that act as servants to families, passed down through generations, and the *domovoi* of Slavic folklore, so the ghost can be enslaved.

And finally, there are the various forms of *hantu*. There's the *hantu raya* (translated as "great ghost"), which is a worker ghost; like the bajang and the pelesit, it is a servant, and it takes on the appearance of its controller. This kind of ghost is forced to stay close to home. Then there's the *hantu air*, which are water spirits that live in rivers or large lakes, often ghosts of those who have drowned in those bodies of water, but not necessarily (see those water spirits of European folklore). They have been known to take on the appearance of a floating log to drown or eat people. The *hantu laut* (the sea spirits) are sympathetic to fishermen and sailors and help them in their time of need. Then there's the *hantu galah*, which is a female and haunts forests and bamboo groves. This kind of ghost is generally very thin and tall.

And finally, there's the *hantu bungkus* (also known as the *pocong*), which are the corpses for whom the proper rituals have not been conducted. For these bodies, the problem is the white shroud. At the burial, the shroud should be untied, and if it is not, the body becomes a pocong, without a true mind, and feeds on the blood of babies. They are a form of vampire ghost.

The white lady myth that we mentioned in the chapter covering the Americas—that is, the story of a woman dressed in a white shroud who appears out of nowhere and often seems to warn of an impending danger, only to disappear afterward—can be found all over the world, but the myth is very popular in the Philippines. White lady sightings are common throughout the country, and each town and area has its own specific story. Where the legend of the white lady originated in this region, we have a few guesses. The most logical involves the overlaying of Christianity on the regional folklore, resulting in a variation of Virgin Mary sightings.

**Consider This:** Which of these ghost myths you've read here seem to be the closest to what you grew up with, even though you didn't necessarily grow up in that region?

## Summary
*Where Ghosts Are Here and There*
*(Yes, Everywhere!)*

There's one thing we can conclude from this particular trip around the world: ghosts, or at least ghost myths, are everywhere. But then, as we mentioned at the beginning, where there is death of any kind, there are ghost myths. And where there are the dead, there is the living grieving, and there is the never-ending desire to speak with those gone ahead.

There are and have always been those who claim to be able to communicate with them. So there have been mediums and shamans and psychics and even the stories, like that of Orpheus in Greece and the Ghost Camp in North America among the Piegans, and in Africa, the Wachaga story about how a girl reached the land of the ghosts and the Bapedi tale of the man who found his way to the underworld, of those who can straddle the divide and are truly a case of a fish out of water story. Can the spirit communicators do the job that they say they can? That's up to you to decide. Not only that, as we've discovered, where there are ghosts, there are similar themes all over.

Now that you're thinking about it, consider all the

water-related themes when it comes to ghosts, rivers to cross for the deceased to reach the afterworld. And of course, think of the funeral rites (which are important, as we've seen all over the world. Never forget the funeral rites!).

When there is life, there is death, and there is, as always, the sense of wonder. Once more, we are confronted with the realization that we know little. We can barely comprehend the living; how can we say we can comprehend the dead? Study and consider the tales around the world, and draw your own conclusions.

# Bibliography


Appiah, Kwame Anthony, and Henry Louis Gates Jr. [1996]. *Dictionary of Global Culture*, Borzoi Books: Alfred A. Knopf, Inc.

Arrowsmith, Nancy, and George Morse [1977]. *A Field Guide to the Little People*, Macmillan.

Ashe, Geoffrey [1985]. *The Discovery of King Arthur*, Anchor Press/Doubleday.

Bradley, Åsa Maria [2015]. *Viking Warrior Rising*, Sourcebooks.

Briggs, Katharine [1977]. *British Folktales*, Pantheon Books.

Campbell, Joseph [1988]. *Myths to Live By*, Bantam Books.

Cavendish, Richard, ed. [1970]. *Man, Myth & Magic: An Illustrated Encyclopedia of the Supernatural*, Marshall Cavendish Corp.

Conway, D.J. [2001]. *Magickal, Mystical Creatures*, Llewellyn Publications.

Cotterell, Arthur [1996]. *Illustrated Encyclopedia of Classical Mythology*, Hermes House.

Curran, Bob [2009]. *Werewolves*, New Page Books.

Curtis, Vesta Sarkhosh [1933]. *Persian Myths*, University of Texas Press.

Davis, F. Hadland [1989]. *Myths & Legends of Japan*, Graham Brash Ltd.

Davisson, Zack [2017]. *Supernatural Cats of Japan*, Chin Music Press.

Flynn, Elizabeth MS [2017]. "Lafcadio Hearn: The Man Behind the Plaque," Noladefender.com, July 7.

Foster, Michael Dylan [2015]. *The Book of Yokai: Mysterious*

*Creatures of Japanese Folklore*, University of California Press.

Fuller, Edmund [1974]. *Mythology by Thomas Bulfinch*, Dell Publishing.

Graves, Robert [1960]. *The Greek Myths*, Pelican.

Hamel, Frank [2007]. *Werewolves, Bird-Women, Tiger-Men and Other Human Animals*, Dover Publications.

Hamilton, Edith [1969]. *Mythology*, Warner Books.

Haughton, Brian [2008]. *Lore of the Ghost: The Origins of the Most Famous Stories Throughout the World*, New Page Books.

Hearn, Lafcadio [2007]. *Chita: A Memory of Last Island*, Echo Library.

_______ [1971]. *In Ghostly Japan*, Charles E. Tuttle Co.

_______ [2005]. *Kwaidan: Stories and Studies of Strange Things.* Boston: Tuttle.

_______ [2011]. *La Cuisine Creole: A Collection of Culinary Recipes*, Applewood Books.

Ions, Veronica [1992]. *Indian Mythology*, Reed International Books.

Iwasaka, Michiko, and Barre Toelken [1994]. *Ghosts and the Japanese: Cultural Experience in Japanese Death Legends*, Utah State University, University Libraries.

Katz, Brian P. [1995]. *Deities and Demons of the Far East*, MetroBooks.

Knight, Sirona [2005]. *Complete Idiot's Guide to Elves and Fairies*, Penguin Group.

Koizumi, Setsu [1918]. *Reminiscences of Lafcadio Hearn.* New York: Macmillan. Translated by Paul Kiyoshi Hisada and Frederick Johnson.

Matthews, John [1999]. *The Barefoot Book of Giants, Ghosts, and Goblins*, Barefoot Books.

McCoy, Edain [2006]. *A Witch's Guide to Faery Folk*, Llewellyn Publications.

Murray, Alexander S. [1988]. *Who's Who in Mythology: A*

*Classic Guide to the Ancient World*, Bracken Books.
*Mythical Beasts* [1996]. Anness Publishing, Ltd.
Sister Nivedita and Ananda K. Coomararswamy [1994]. *Hindus and Buddhists: Myths and Legends*, Guernsey Press.
Ralston, W.R.S. [1873]. *Russian Folk-Tales*, Elder and Co.
Schama, Simon [2000]. *A History of Britain: At the Edge of the World? 3000 BC to AD 1603*, Hyperion.
Storm, Rachel [2002]. *Asian Mythology*, Selectabook Ltd.
Wikipedia. Various entries.
Wilkinson, Philip [1998]. *Illustrated Dictionary of Mythology*, DK Publishing.
Yoda, Hiroko, and Matt Alt, translators [2016]. *Japandemonium Illustrated: The Yokai Encyclopedias of Toriyama Sekien*, Dover Publications.

# Illustrations

Page 2: Silk Road map. Shutterstock
Page 6: Dover Publications
Page 10: Courtesy of Classic Media
Page 24: Warpaths2peacepipes.com
Page 36: Clip art
Page 54: ClipartXtras
Page 60: Clipartpanda.com
Page 66: Drawn from a photograph of a hieroglyph
Page 72: Demonic ghost, taken from *Thakurmar Jhuli* (1907). Creative Commons license
Page 76: Dover Publications

# Author Biographies

JACQUIE ROGERS is a multiple award–winning author of Western novels, but her first burning desire was to be a baseball announcer. While she hasn't made that career change happen yet, she *has* been a programmer, a cow milker, a political strategist, a rodeo queen, and a bookstore manager, but currently, she writes stories about another place, another time. Check them out at JacquieRogers.com!

ELIZABETH MS FLYNN, who writes as Eilis Flynn, has written fiction in the form of comic book stories, fantasies (romance, urban, and historical), and short stories. She's also a professional editor and has been for more than forty years, working with academia, technology, finance, genre fiction, and comic books. She can be reached at emsflynn.com (if you're looking for an editor) or at eilisflynn.com (if you're looking for a good read).

# Connect with us online

Facebook: www.facebook.com/jacquie.rogers.author

Facebook: www.facebook.com/EilisFlynnAuthor

Jacquie Rogers's website: www.jacquierogers.com
Eilis Flynn's website: www.eilisflynn.com

**Have any ghost stories you want to share? Have any questions? Drop by at mythsalongthesilkroad.blogspot.com!**